CURRENT PROBLEMS IN SECURITY ANALYSIS

BY

BENJAMIN GRAHAM

Chairman of Security Analysis Department, New York Institute of Finance
Co-author, "Security Analysis" by Graham & Dodd

Transcripts of Lectures
September, 1946 — February, 1947

PART I

Martino Publishing
Mansfield Centre, CT
2010

Martino Publishing
P.O. Box 373,
Mansfield Centre, CT 06250 USA

www.martinopublishing.com

ISBN 1-57898-955-8

Cover design by T. Matarazzo

Printed in the United States of America On 100% Acid-Free Paper

CURRENT PROBLEMS IN SECURITY ANALYSIS

BY

BENJAMIN GRAHAM

Chairman of Security Analysis Department, New York Institute of Finance
Co-author, "Security Analysis" by Graham & Dodd

Transcripts of Lectures
September, 1946 — February, 1947

PART I

NEW YORK INSTITUTE OF FINANCE
Publishing Division
20 BROAD STREET   NEW YORK 5, N. Y.

NEW YORK INSTITUTE OF FINANCE
20 Broad Street New York City

Transcripts of Lectures
"CURRENT PROBLEMS IN SECURITY ANALYSIS"

BY

BENJAMIN GRAHAM

WARNING

The following transcripts of Mr. Graham's
lectures on "Current Problems in Security Analysis" contain references to specific companies
and securities. These references are for illustrative purposes only, and no attempt has been
made to provide all the facts pertinent to a
thorough analysis. Any mention of securities is
not to be construed as a suggestion to invest or
speculate in same.

Neither the New York Institute of Finance
nor Mr. Graham assume any responsibility for loss
resulting from action taken because of any statement contained in these lecture transcripts.

ALBERT P. SQUIER, DIRECTOR
NEW YORK INSTITUTE OF FINANCE

Price - ███ per set of transcripts of ten lectures.
$5.00

NEW YORK INSTITUTE OF FINANCE
Publishing Division
20 Broad Street   New York 5, N.Y.

NEW YORK INSTITUTE OF FINANCE
20 Broad Street New York City

Lecture No. 1   September 24, 1946

CURRENT PROBLEMS IN SECURITY ANALYSIS

By
Benjamin Graham
****

May I welcome you all to this series of lectures. The
large enrollment is quite a compliment to the Institute, and
perhaps to the lecturer; but it also poses something of a problem.
We shall not be able to handle this course on an informal or
round-table basis. However, I should like to welcome as much
discussion and as many intelligent questions as we can get, but
I shall have to reserve the right to cut short discussion or not
to answer questions in the interest of getting along with the
course. You all understand our problem, I am sure.

I hope you will find that your time and money will be
profitably spent in this course; but I want to add that the
purpose of this course is to provide illustrative examples and
discussions only, and not to supply practical ideas for security
market operations. We assume no responsibility for anything
said along the latter lines in this course; and so far as our
own business is concerned we may or we may not have an interest
in any of the securities that are mentioned and discussed. That
is also a teaching problem with which we have been familiar
through the years, and we want to get it behind us as soon as
we can.

The subject of this course is "Current Problems in
Security Analysis", and that covers a pretty wide field.
Actually, the idea is to attempt to bring our textbook "Security
Analysis", up to date, in the light of the experience of the last
six years since the 1940 revision was published.

The subject matter of security analysis can be divided
in various ways. One division might be in three parts: First,
the techniques of security analysis; secondly, standards of
safety and common stock valuation; and thirdly, the relationship
of the analyst to the security market.

Another way of dividing the subject might be to
consider, first, the analyst as an investigator, in which role
he gathers together all the relevant facts and serves them up
in the most palatable and illuminating fashion he can. And then
to consider the analyst as a judge of values, or an evaluator.
This first division of the subject is rather useful, I think,
because there is a good field in Wall Street for people whose

work it will be mainly to digest the facts, and to abstain from passing judgment on the facts, leaving that to other people.

Such sticking to the facts alone might be very salutary; for the judgment of security analysts on securities is so much influenced by market conditions down here that most of us are not able, I fear, to express valuation judgments as good analysts. We find ourselves almost always acting as a mixture of market experts and security experts. I had hoped that there would be some improvement in that situation over the years, but I must confess that I haven't seen a great deal of it. Analysts have recently been acting in Wall Street pretty much as they always have, that is to say, with one eye on the balance sheet and income account, and the other eye on the stock ticker.

It might be best in this introductory lecture to deal with the third aspect of the security analyst's work, and that is his relationship to the security market. It is a little more interesting, perhaps, than the other subdivisions, and I think it is relevant as introductory material.

The correct attitude of the security analyst toward the stock market might well be that of a man toward his wife. He shouldn't pay too much attention to what the lady says, but he can't afford to ignore it entirely. That is pretty much the position that most of us find ourselves vis-a-vis the stock market.

When we consider how the stock market has acted in the last six years, we shall conclude that it has acted pretty much as one would expect it to, based upon past experience. To begin with, it has gone up and it has gone down, and different securities have acted in different fashion. We have tried to illustrate this simply, by indicating on the blackboard the behavior of some sample stocks since the end of 1938. Let me take occasion to point out some of the features in this record that may interest security analysts.

There are two elements of basic importance, I think, that the analyst should recognize in the behavior of stocks over the last six years. The first is the principle of continuity, and the other is what I would call the principle of deceptive selectivity in the stock market.

First, with regard to continuity: The extraordinary thing about the securities market, if you judge it over a long period of years, is the fact that it does not go off on tangents permanently, but it remains in a continuous orbit. When I say that it doesn't go off on tangents, I mean the simple point that after the stock market goes up a great deal it not only comes down a great deal but it comes down to levels to which we had previously been accustomed. Thus we have never found the stock market as a whole going off into new areas and staying there permanently because there has been a permanent change in the basic

conditions. I think you would have expected such new departures
in stock prices. For the last thirty years, the period of time
that I have watched the securities market, we have had two world
wars; we have had a tremendous boom and a tremendous deflation;
we now have the Atomic Age on us. Thus you might well assume
that the security market could really have been permanently
transformed at one time or another, so that the past records
might not have been very useful in judging future values.

            Actually that hasn't happened. I don't know why it
hasn't happened and I am sure I can't guarantee that it won't
happen in the future. But I think our experience of the
continuity of the market over so long a time and under such
extraordinary conditions would make it sensible for the security
analyst to assume that it will continue until he is convinced
by very careful reasoning of his own that we really are going
to be in a new world of security values.

            These remarks are relevant, of course, to developments
since 1940. When the security market advanced in the last few
years to levels which were not unexampled but which were high
in relation to past experience, there was a general tendency for
security analysts to assume that a new level of values had been
established for stock prices which was quite different from
those we had previously been accustomed to. It may very well be
that individual stocks have now entered a new situation which
carries them completely away from what they were before; and it
may well be also that stocks as a whole are worth more than they
used to be. But the thing that doesn't seem to be true is that
they are worth so much more than they used to be that past
experience--i.e., past levels and patterns of behavior--can be
discarded.

            One way of expressing the principle of continuity in
concrete terms would be as follows: When you look at the stock
market as a whole, you will find from experience that after it
has advanced a good deal it not only goes down -- that is obvious--
but it goes down to levels substantially below earlier high levels.
Hence it has always been possible to buy stocks at lower prices
than the highest of previous moves, not of the current move. That
means, in short, that the investor who says he does not wish
to buy securities at high levels, because they don't appeal to
him on a historical basis or on an analytical basis, can point
to past experience to warrant the assumption that he will have
an opportunity to buy them at lower prices--not only lower than
current high prices, but lower than previous high levels. In
sum, therefore, you can take previous high levels, if you wish,
as a measure of the danger point in the stock market for
investors, and I think you will find that past experience would
bear you out using this as a practical guide. Thus, if you look
at this chart of the Dow Jones Industrial Average, you can see
there has never been a time in which the price level has broken
out, in a once-for-all or permanent way, from its past area of

fluctuations.   That is the thing I have been trying to point out
in the last few minutes.

          Another way of illustrating the principle of continuity
is by looking at the long-term earnings of the Dow-Jones
Industrial Average. We have figures here running back to 1915,
which is more than thirty years, and it is extraordinary to see
the persistence with which the earnings of the Dow Jones
Industrial Average return to a figure of about $10 per unit.
It is true that they got away from it repeatedly.   In 1917,
for example, they got up to $22 a unit; but in 1921 they earned
nothing. And a few years later they were back to $10.   In 1915
the earnings of the unit were $10.59; in 1945 they were prac-
tically the same. All of the changes in between appear to have
been merely of fluctuations around the central figure. So much
for this idea of continuity?

          The second thing that I want to talk about is
selectivity. Here is an idea that has misled security analysts
and advisers to a very great extent. In the few weeks preceding
the recent break in the stock market I noticed that a great many
of the brokerage house advisers were saying that now that the
market has ceased to go up continuously, the thing to do is to
exercise selectivity in your purchases; and in that way you can
still derive benefits from security price changes. Well, it
stands to reason that if you define selectivity as picking out
a stock which is going to go up a good deal later on--or more
than the rest--you are going to benefit. But that is too obvious
a definition. What the commentators mean, as is evident from
their actual arguments, is that if you buy the securities which
apparently have good earnings prospects, you will then benefit
market-wise; whereas if you buy the others you won't.

          History shows this to be a very plausible idea but
an extremely misleading one; that is why I referred to this
concept of selectivity as deceptive. One of the easiest ways to
illustrate that is by taking two securities here in the Dow-Jones
Average, National Distillers and United Aircraft. You will find
that National Distillers sold at lower average prices in 1940-1942
than in 1935-1939. No doubt there was a general feeling that
the company's prospects were not good, primarily because it was
thought that war would not be a very good thing for a luxury
type of business such as whiskey is politely considered to be.

          In the same way you will find that the United Aircraft
Company through 1940-1942, was better regarded than the average
stock, because it was thought that here was a company that had
especially good prospects of making money; and so it did. But
if you had bought and sold these securities, as most people seem
to have done, on the basis of these obvious differential prospects,
you would have made a complete error. For, as you see, National
Distillers went up from the low of 1940 more than fivefold
recently, and is now selling nearly four times its 1940 price.

The buyer of United Aircraft would have had a very small profit
at its best price and would now have a loss of one third of his
money.

This principle of selectivity can be explored in
various other ways. Let us show it by reference to American Can
and American Woolen, because that comparison can carry us back to
the first World War, with some very interesting results.

During the early part of the late war American Woolen
was obviously not well regarded: it was a poor stock to begin with,
selling at a few dollars a share--let us say $9.50 in 1939--and
in the 1942 low it went down to $3.50. If you had spoken about
selectivity as represented by the customary ideas of the stock
market, American Woolen would have been considered as very
unattractive in 1942. But you all know, it had a spectacular
rise in 1945 to 70 3/4; and it is now selling at 40, which is
about ten times its 1942 low.

American Can, on the other hand, had no advance
to speak of from its 1939 average price to its 1946 high, and
is now selling at lower prices than it sold in 1938 and 1939.
The market presumably is here saying American Woolen has relatively
good prospects over the years to come. American Can presumably
is not as attractive as it used to be, since its price is lower
than the 1938-39 average; whereas the Dow-Jones price as a whole
is higher than the 1938-39 average. But these judgments of the
market are based upon rather obvious facts that the woolen
industry has become very prosperous during recent years, while the
canning industry has been held down because it was already very
prosperous and it gave up nearly all its extra earnings in the
form of excess profits taxes.

If you go back to the last war you will find some very
interesting figures on American Can and American Woolen. I want
to give them to you here, because I am more and more convinced
that a good security analyst goes up and down through time in his
analysis, and that he doesn't limit himself to the situation as
it appears to be at the single moment at which he is studying
a situation.

Now let me give you this brief resume of what happened
to American Can and American Woolen from before the first World
War to about the present time: The average price in 1911-13 was
the same for both companies--about $25 a share. They both advanced
about the same amount in the bull market of 1916-17. They both
declined in 1918 by approximately the same amount. In 1919, when
the postwar bull market came into effect--which was based largely
upon inflationary moves in commodities--American Can advanced to
69 and American Woolen advanced to 170. You will remember both
of them started from 25. Thus the market believed in 1919 that
American Woolen was a very much better company than American Can.

When the collapse came in that market in 1920-21, you
might think then that the market would have seen the error of
its ways, in these two companies, and would have made American
Woolen decline very much more than American Can. That is not so.
American Can declined to 22 in 1920, which meant it lost more
than two thirds of its value, and American Woolen declined to
56, which was just about the same proportion. You ended up the
postwar rise and the postwar decline of 1919-1921 in somewhat
the same way as you did in 1938-1946--namely, with American Woolen
showing a considerably better price than it started with, and
American Can selling lower than it started with. (We are assuming
for the moment that the 1946 prices that we are now pointing
to on the Board are the lows for the current postwar recession.)

In other words, the market in the first World War, basing
its ideas upon the behavior of these two companies during the
war and its concept of their prospects, decided that American
Woolen was more than twice as good as American Can after the war
was over and in the midst of the postwar recession. Well, the
subsequent market history is extraordinary. American Can advanced
to the equivalent price of about $1,000 a share in 1929, allowing
for break-ups; but American Woolen in 1929 sold at a considerably
lower price than it did in 1919. I think its high price in the
1929 boom was $28 a share, which was one half its low price
in the 1920 depression. Thus we see that the true prospects of
these two companies, as we now measure them retrospectively, were
as completely different as you can imagine from the prospects as
they were gauged by the market, both in the rise of 1919 and the
decline of 1920.

Another point about American Woolen that is rather
interesting is the change in its working capital, because it
is extraordinary how figures repeat themselves in Wall Street
experience. Before World War I, American Woolen's working capital
was 22 1/2 million dollars. At the end of 1921 it was 62 million
dollars, showing the great advantage from the war. By the end
of 1938, when the stock was selling at $7, the working capital had
shrunk to 30 million. Now, as a result of the second war, in
June 1946 it is back again to 64 million dollars--this being partly
the reason for the great enthusiasm that was reflected in the rise
to $70 in 1946.

Now, my point in going at these two things in such
detail is to try to bring home to you the fact that what seems
to be obvious and simple to the people in Wall Street, as well as
to their customers, is not really obvious and simple at all.
You are not going to get good results in security analysis by
doing the simple, obvious thing of picking out the companies
that apparently have good prospects--whether it be the automobile
industry, or the building industry, or any such combination of
companies which almost everybody can tell you are going to enjoy
good business for a number of years to come. That method is just
too simple and too obvious--and the main fact about it is that it

does not work well. The method of selectivity which I believe
does work well is one that is based on demonstrated value
differentials representing the application of security analysis
techniques which have been well established and well tested.
These techniques frequently yield indications that a security is
undervalued, or at least that it is definitely more attractive
than other securities may be, with which it is compared.

    As an example of that kind of thing, I might take the
comparisons that were made in the Security Analysis*, 1940 edition,
between three groups of common stocks. They were compared as of
the end of 1938, or just before the war. Of these groups one
contained common stocks said to be speculative because their
price was high; the second contained those said to be speculative
because of their irregular record; and the third contained those
said to be attractive investments because they met investment
tests from a quantitative standpoint. Let me now mention the
names of the stocks, and indicate briefly what is their position
as of today. Group A consisted of General Electric, Coca-Cola,
and Johns-Manville. Their combined price at the end of 1938
was $281, and at recent lows it was $303.50, which meant that
they have advanced 8 per cent.

    The second group (about which we expressed no real
opinion except that they could not be analyzed very well) sold
in the aggregate for 124 at the end of 1938 and at recent lows
for 150, which was an advance of 20 per cent.

    The three stocks which were said to be attractive
investments from the quantitative standpoint sold at 70 1/2 at
the end of 1938--that is for one share of each--and their value
at the recent lows was 207, or an increase of 190 per cent.

    Of course, these performances may be just a coincidence.
You can't prove a principle by one or two examples. But I think
it is a reasonably good illustration of the results which you
should get on the average by using investment tests of merit,
as distinct from the emphasis on general prospects which plays
so great a part in most of the analysis that I see around the
Street.

    I would like to pause now for any questions on these
two matters of continuity and selectivity. I have at the bottom
of the list here prices which some of you can't see. This is a
similar record of Intertype--which you may recall was one of the
companies which, in our textbook, we indicated was probably
undervalued by an analyst's tests, at the end of 1939, but which
the market did not like because it represented a secondary type
of business without any special glamour. The figures which we
show here indicate that the high price in 1938 was 12 3/4; the
low price in 1940 was 5 1/4; the high price in 1946 was 34 1/2;
and the current price is 21, which of course represents a
    *"Security Analysis" by Graham & Dodd.

substantially better rise than that of the Dow-Jones stocks as a whole.

Intertype, I think, is characteristic of a very large number of securities, the market position of which has been quite revolutionized in the last six years. It is extraordinary how the attitude of the public has changed with regard to secondary stocks. In 1940 you had to wage a great campaign to interest anybody in stocks of this kind, even though they could be bought at one half of their working capital and even though they had earnings of very substantial amounts in relation to the price.

At the top of 1946 most of the secondary stocks were selling at extremely high multiples of their average earnings prewar. For example, if we take Intertype (which, remember, was one of the attractive issues from our analytical standpoint a few years ago, which meant that it made a better showing than the typical secondary issue), we find that in the five years ended 1940 it earned $1.05 per share and in the five years ended 1945 it earned $1.53. At the high price of 34 1/2 it was selling at more than thirty times its prewar earnings and more than twenty times its war earnings. That, I would say, is quite typical of a large group of secondary stocks.

If we ask, "On what basis could securities of that kind have been recommended at such prices?"--and I presume, in fact I know, that many of them were recommended -- the answer is that it was expected that in the postwar period these companies would do very well because of the large demand for their products.

One point I want to raise in that connection, which I believe is vital in the thinking of analysts, is how a security analyst can reconcile himself to a complete about-face on the underlying character of a group of stocks, merely because special and non-recurrent influences have come into play. Why should Intertype now have become an attractive kind of company to invest in, when a few years before it was regarded by the majority of people who looked at it as a basically unattractive kind of company? I submit that very little thorough thinking had been done on the question whether the underlying nature of that business--and of that whole group of companies similar thereto-- had changed merely because they have had a relatively favorable earnings experience during the war.

A point that was mentioned now and then in brokerage circulars, but has never been brought home properly, is the fact that the earnings of these secondary companies under war conditions (and under immediate postwar conditions) were gained in the absence of any competition for markets. Thus they were able to sell their product merely because they could turn it out. It would seem to me that an analyst who had some idea of the past position of these companies would have stressed very greatly the question how they would fare when real competition for sales is resumed. It may be that Wall Street analysts have been under the impression that there never would be a resumption of competition for sales. It is hard for me to believe that. I don't think they have any such conviction. I believe they preferred not even to think about that question, although it was their duty to consider it.

I want to pass on finally to the most vulnerable position of the securities market in the recent rise, and that is the area of new common stock offerings. The aggregate amount of these offerings has not been very large in hundreds of millions of dollars, because the typical company involved was comparatively small. But I think the effect of these offerings upon the position of people in Wall Street was quite significant, because all of these offerings were bought by people who, I am quite sure, didn't know what they were doing and were thus subject to very sudden changes of heart and attitude with regard to their investments. If you made any really careful study of the typical offerings that we have seen in the last twelve months you will agree, I am sure, with a statement made (only in a footnote unfortunately) by the Securities and Exchange Commission on August 20, 1946. They say that: "The rapidity with which many new securities, whose evident hazards are plainly stated in a registration statement and prospectus, are gobbled up at prices far exceeding any reasonable likelihood of return gives ample evidence that the prevalent demand for securities includes a marked element of blind recklessness. Registration cannot cure that."

That is true. Among the astonishing things is the fact that the poorer the security the higher relatively was the price it was sold at. The reason is that most of the sounder securities had already been sold to and held by the public, and their market price was based on ordinary actions of buyers and sellers. The market price of the new securities has been largely determined, I think, by the fact that security salesmen could sell any security at any price; and there was therefore a tendency for the prices to be higher for these new securities than for others of better quality.

I think it is worth while giving you a little resume of one of the most recent prospectuses, which is summarized in the Standard Corporation Record of September 13, about a week ago. I don't think this stock was actually sold, but it was intended to be sold at $16 a share. The name of the company is the Northern Engraving and Manufacturing Company, and we have this simple set-up: There are 250,000 shares to be outstanding, some of which are to be sold at $16 for the account of stockholders. That meant that this company was to be valued at four million dollars in the market.

Now, what did the new stockholder get for his share of the four million dollars? In the first place, he got $1,350,000 worth of tangible equity. Hence he was paying three times the

amount of money invested in the business. In the second place,
he got earnings which can be summarized rather quickly. For the
five years 1936-40, they averaged 21¢ a share; for the five years
ended 1945, they averaged 65¢ a share. In other words, the stock
was beingsold at about twenty-five times the prewar earnings.
But naturally there must have been some factor that made such a
thing possible, and we find it in the six months ending June 30,
1946, when the company earned $1.27 a share. In the usual
parlance of Wall Street, it could be said that the stock was
being sold at 6 1/2 times its earnings, the point being the
earnings are at the annual rate of $2.54, and $16 is six or seven
times that much.

        It is bad enough, of course, to offer to the public
anything on the basis of a six months' earnings figure alone,
when all the other figures make the price appear so extraordinarily
high. But in this case it seems to me the situation is
extraordinary in another respect--that is in relation to the
nature of the business. The company manufactures metal name-
plates, dials, watch-dials, panels, etc. The products are made
only against purchase contracts and are used by manufacturers
of motors, controls, and equipment, and so forth.

        Now, we don't stress industrial analysis particularly
in our course in security analysis, and I am not going to stress
it here. But we have to assume that the security analyst has a
certain amount of business sense. Surely he would ask himself,
"How much profit can a company make in this line of business--
operating on purchase contracts with automobile and other
manufacturers--in relation both to its invested capital and its
sales?"

        In the six months ended June 1946 the company earned
15 per cent on its sales after taxes. It had previously tended
to earn somewhere around 3 or 4 per cent on sales after taxes.
It seems to me anyone would know that these earnings for the
six months arose from the fact that any product could be sold
provided only it could be turned out, and that extremely high
profits could be realized in this kind of market. I think it
would have been evident that under more sound conditions this is
the kind of business which is doomed to earn a small profit margin
on its sales and only a moderate amount on its net worth, for
it has nothing particular to offer except the know-how to turn
out relatively small gadgets for customer buyers.

        That, I believe, illustates quite well what the
public had been offered in this recent new security market.
There are countless other illustrations that I could give. I
would like to mention one that is worth referring to, I think,
because of its contrast with other situations.

        The Taylorcraft Company is a maker of small airplanes.
In June, 1946, they sold 20,000 shares of stock to the public

at $13, the company getting $11: and then they voted a four-for-
one split up. The stock is now quoted around 2 1/2 or 2 3/4,
the equivalent of about $11 for the stock that was sold.

If you look at the Taylorcraft Company, you find some
rather extraordinary things in its picture. To begin with, the
company is today selling for about three million dollars, and this
is supposedly in a rather weak market. The working capital shown
as of June 30, 1946, is only $103,000. It is able to show even
that much working capital first, after including the proceeds of
the sale of this stock, and secondly, after not showing as a
current liability an excess profits tax of $196,000 which they are
trying to avoid by means of a "Section 722" claim. Well,
practically every corporation that I know of has filed Section 722
claims to try to cut down their excess profits taxes. This is
the only corporation I know of that, on the strength of filing
that claim, does not show its excess profits tax as a current
liability.

They also show advances payable, due over one year, of
$130,000, which of course don't have to be shown as current
liabilities. Finally, the company shows $2,300,000 for stock and
surplus, which is not as much as the market price of the stock.
But even here we note that the plant was marked up by $1,150,000,
so that just about half of the stock and surplus is represented
by what I would call an arbitrary plant mark-up.

Now, there are several other interesting things about
the Taylorcraft Company itself, and there are still other things
even more interesting when you compare it with other aircraft
companies. For one thing, the Taylorcraft Company did not publish
reports for a while and it evidently was not in too comfortable a
financial position. Thus it arranged to sell these shares of
stock in an amount which did not require registration with the
SEC. But it is also a most extraordinary thing for a company in
bad financial condition to arrange to sell stock to tide it over,
and at the same time to arrange to split up its stock four for
one. That kind of operation -- to split a stock from $11 to
$3 -- seems to me to be going pretty far in the direction of
trading on the most unintelligent elements in Wall Street
stock purchasing that you can find.

But the really astonishing thing is to take Taylorcraft
and compare it, let us say, with another company like Curtiss-
Wright. Before the split-up, Taylorcraft and Curtiss-Wright
apparently were selling about the same price, but that doesn't
mean very much. The Curtiss-Wright Company is similar to United
Aircraft in that its price is now considerably lower than its
1939 average. The latter was 8 3/4, and its recent price was
5 3/4. In the meantime, the Curtiss-Wright Company has built up
its working capital from a figure perhaps of 12 million dollars
to 130 million dollars, approximately. It turns out that this
company is selling in the market for considerably less than two
thirds of its working capital.

The Curtiss-Wright Company happens to be the largest
airplane producer in the field, and the Taylorcraft Company
probably is one of the smallest. There are sometimes advantages
in small size and disadvantages in large size; but it is hard to
believe that a small company in a financially weak position can
be worth a great deal more than its tangible investment, when the
largest companies in the same field are selling at very large
discounts from their working capital.

During the period in which Taylorcraft was marking up
its fixed assets by means of this appraisal figure, the large
companies like United Aircraft and Curtiss-Wright marked down
their plants to practically nothing, although the number of
square feet which they owned was tremendous. So you have exactly
the opposite situation in those two types of companies.

The contrast that I am giving you illustrates to my
mind not only the obvious abuses of the securities market in
the last two years, but it also illustrates the fact that the
security analyst can in many cases come to pretty definite
conclusions that one security is relatively unattractive and
other securities are attractive. I think the same situation
exists in today's market as has existed in security markets
always, namely, that there are great and demonstrable discrepancies
in value--not in the majority of cases, but in enough cases to
make this work interesting for the security analyst.

When I mentioned Curtiss-Wright selling at two thirds
or less of its working capital alone, my mind goes back again to
the last war; and I think this might be a good point more or less
to close on, because it gives you an idea of the continuity of
the security markets.

During the last war, when you were just beginning with
airplanes, the Wright Aeronautical Company was the chief factor
in that business, and it did pretty well in its small way,
earning quite a bit of money. In 1922 nobody seemed to have any
confidence in the future of the Wright Aeronautical Company. Some
of you will remember our reference to it in Security Analysis.
That stock sold then at $8 a share, when its working capital was
about $18 a share at the time. Presumably "the market" felt that
its prospects were very unattractive. That stock subsequently,
as you may know, advanced to $280 a share.

Now it is interesting to see Curtiss-Wright again,
after World War II, being regarded as presumably a completely
unattractive company. For it is selling again at only a small
percentage of its asset value, in spite of the fact that it has
earned a great deal of money. I am not predicting that Curtiss-
Wright will advance in the next ten years the way Wright
Aeronautical did after 1922. The odds are very much against it.
Because, if I remember my figures, Wright Aeronautical had only
about 250,000 shares in 1922 and Curtiss-Wright has about

7,250,000 shares, which is a matter of great importance. But
it is interesting to see how unpopular companies can become,
merely because their immediate prospects are clouded in the
speculative mind.

I want to say one other thing about the Curtiss-Wright
picture, which leads us over into the field of techniques of
analysis, about which I intend to speak at the next session. When
you study the earnings of Curtiss-Wright in the last ten years,
you will find that the earnings shown year by year are quite good;
but the true earnings have been substantially higher still,
because of the fact that large reserves were charged off against
these earnings which have finally appeared in the form of current
assets in the balance sheet. That point is one of great
importance in the present-day technique of analysis.

In analyzing a company's showing over the war period
it is quite important that you should do it by the balance sheet
method, or at least use the balance sheet as a check. That is
to say, subtract the balance sheet value shown at the beginning
from that at the end of the period, and add back the dividends.
Thus sum--adjusted for capital transactions--will give you the
earnings that were actually realized by the company over the
period. In the case of Curtiss-Wright we have as much as 44
million dollars' difference between the earnings as shown by the
single reports and the earnings as shown by a comparison of
surplus and reserves at the beginning and end of the period.
These excess or unrevealed earnings alone are more than $6 a
share on the stock, which is selling today at only about that
figure.

To illustrate that method of analysis in the next
session, I shall present several of such balance sheet comparisons.
That, I believe, you may find of great value in your work in
current security analysis.

Are there any questions to be asked before we adjourn
this class? If not, I will meet you all again on October 8 for
our second session.

Lecture No. 2   October 8, 1946.

CURRENT PROBLEMS IN SECURITY ANALYSIS

By
Benjamin Graham
****

        Today I want to discuss that portion of the security
analyst's approach in reaching conclusions as to future prospects
as would be derived from the company's past record.

        I mentioned in the last lecture that we now have
available for the study of each enterprise a ten-year period
which divides itself naturally into two parts: 1936-1940,
representing the pre-war period, perhaps slightly overstated
because of the inclusion of 1940; and 1941-45, definitely the
war period. But in addition to breaking down earnings as reported
into these two segments for further study, it is quite interesting
and valuable to review the period from the standpoint of balance
sheet analysis.

        Those of you who are familiar with our textbook know
that we recommend "the comparative balance sheet approach" for
various reasons, one of which is to obtain a check on the
reported earnings. In the war period just finished that is
particularly important because the reported earnings have been
affected by a number of abnormal influences, the true nature of
which can be understood only by a study of balance sheet developments.

        I have put on the blackboard a simple comparative example
to illustrate this point. It is not particularly spectacular.
It occurred to me because I observed that early this year
Transue Williams and Buda Company both sold at the same high
price, namely $33 1/2 a share; and in studying the companies'
record I could see that buyers could easily have been misled
by the ordinary procedure of looking at the reported earnings
per share as they appear, let us say, in Standard Statistics
reports.

        Now, as to procedure: First, the balance sheet comparison
is a relatively simple idea. You take the equity for the stock
at the end of the period, you subtract the equity at the beginning
of the period, and the difference is the gain. That gain should
be adjusted for items that do not relate to earnings, and there
should be added back the dividends paid. Then you get the
earnings for the period as shown by the balance sheet.

In the case of Transue Williams the final stock equity was $2,979,000, of which $60,000 had come from the sale of stock, so that the adjusted equity would be $2,919,000. The indicated earnings were $430,000, or 3.17 a share. The transfer to a per share basis can be made at any convenient time that you wish. Dividends added back of 9.15 give you earnings per balance sheet of $12.32. But if you look at the figures that I have in the Standard Statistics reports, you would see that they add up to 14.73 for the ten years, so that the company actually lost $2.41 somewhere along the line.

The Buda situation is the opposite. We can take either the July 31, 1945 date or the July 31, 1946 date. It happens that only yesterday the July 31, 1946 figures came in, but it's a little simpler to consider July 1945 for this purpose.

We find there that the equity increased $4,962,000 or $25.54 per share, the diviends were much less liberal-- $4.20; indicated earnings per balance sheet, $29.74, but in the income account only $24.57. So this company did $5.17 better than it showed, if you assume that the reserves as given in the balance sheet are part of the stockholder's equity and do not constitute a liability of the company?

If you ask the reason for the difference in the results in these two companies, you would find it, of course, in the treatment of the reserve items. The Transue & Williams Company reported earnings after allowances for reserves, chiefly for renegotiation, each year (reserves added up to $1,240,000 for 1942-45) and then almost every year they charged their actual payments on account of renegotiation to the reserves. It turned out that the amounts to be charged were greater than the amounts which they provided. The reserves set up by Transue and Williams, consequently, were necessary reserves for charges that they were going to have to meet; not only were they real, but they actually proved insufficient on the whole. I think I should perhaps correct what I said in this one respect: It may be that Transue and Williams called their reserve a reserve for contingencies, but actually it was a reserve for renegotiation which, as I said, proved insufficient.

In the case of Buda you have the oppositie situation. The Buda Company made very ample provision for renegotiation, which they charged to earnings currently, and in addition to that they set up reserves for contingencies. These apparently did not constitute in any sense real liabilities, because in July 1946 the reserves of a contingency nature remained at about a million dollars.

In the case of Transue, their reserves got up very high but the end of 1945 saw them down to $13,000, which indicated how necessary were the Transue reserves.

Now, let me pause for a moment to see if there is any question in your mind about this explanation as to why you get different earnings on the two bases, and why Buda shows larger earnings than reported and Transue shows smaller earnings than reported. Maybe a question will clarify it.

QUESTION: Does the equity include reserves?

MR. GRAHAM: Yes. That's a good question. By equity we mean common stock plus surplus, plus whatever reserves are regarded as equivalent of surplus. Reserves which are for known liabilities or probable liabilities would, of course, not be part of the equity.

QUESTION: Might not depreciation charges, which make a great deal of difference in what your equity really was, not show up in there?

MR. GRAHAM: That is true. You can very well claim that certain charges for depreciation have created equities for stock which do not appear on the balance sheet, and I will go into that matter later. But that is a separate consideration from this item, in which we deal only with reserves for contingencies and the like. Are there other questions about that?

Now, I have some other examples which I can go through very quickly to indicate more significant differences in the reported earnings, and the actual earnings. They would be found in some of the real "war babies", particularly the aircraft manufacturing companies.

I mentioned last week the case of Curtiss Wright, particularly because its price was statistically so low in relation to its performance in the past and also by comparison with another small company which I mentioned. Now, in the case of Curtiss Wright, if you follow this procedure, you will find that on the balance sheet basis in ten years they apparently earned $18.53 per share but the reported earnings were only $12.28. In other words, an average of $1.22 is reported and $1.84 is shown by the balance sheet figures. That's a very considerable difference,--an increase of fifty per cent. All of those extra earnings of $6.25 in ten years are to be found in the reserves set up during the last five years by the Curtiss Wright Corporation, none of which apparently are needed for specific war purposes, such as renegotiation payments or reconversion expenditures. Actually, the situation is quite the opposite in Curtiss Wright and others of that type. Instead of having to spend a great deal of money on plant in the reconversion period, you found the opposite has proved true. For in going over from war conditions to peace conditions these companies have turned a great deal of plant account into cash, which we will touch upon later.

In the United Aircraft situation you have somewhat the same picture, not as extreme. The reported earnings for ten years were $41.08 and the indicated earnings per balance sheet were $49.84,--a difference of about twenty per cent, or $8.77.

If you look at the balance sheet there you will see that they have set up reserves amounting to $35,000,000 or about $14 a share, and you may ask why the difference in earnings is not equal to the full reserves of $14 per share. Well, if you examine the report in detail you will see that part of those reserves were charged to earnings, and therefore served to decrease the reported earnings, but somewhat less than half, $15,000,000, was taken out of surplus and transferred to reserve. Restoration of this last amount, of course, would not serve to increase your reported earnings, because it was not deducted before arriving at the reported earnings. I hope you are all familiar with the difference between making a charge to reserves which would appear in the income account before your reported earnings, and a charge on the balance sheet only where it is transferred from surplus to reserves. The latter is purely internal, and a matter of no special significance.

These are the examples that I wanted to give you of comparative balance sheets for the purpose of determining what we might call true earnings, as compared with reported earnings. Now, I think we should take a little time to talk about specific factors that entered into these earnings' pictures in the last few years, particularly, of course, the war period. It is essential for a good analyst to know his way around in these company reports, especially where new types of items appear.

One item I have already spoken to you about, and that is renegotiation. There was a great deal of uncertainty about that picture in the corporate report of the early part of the war period. It has now been pretty well cleaned up for all companies, and we know that for the most part the companies have charged adequate amounts for renegotiation in their income accounts. Hence in most cases no special attention has to be given to that feature.

Besides renegotiation we have the contingency reserves situation which, at times, has been confused with renegotiation reserves for a reason that I might point out to you,--which is based on my own experience in renegotiation matters in Washington. Quite a number of companies decided that they would by no means set up anything that they would identify as renegotiation reserves, because they considered that was tantamount to a confession that they would have to give that money back, and they wanted to argue about it before they gave it back. So they made the provision and called it "contingency reserves for postwar occurrences", or almost anything but renegotiation. But we all knew that their auditors had advised them to set up those reserves because they would be needed for renegotiation refunds.

However, besides those contingency items that were not
really contingency reserves, we have had a large number of
miscellaneous reserves for contingencies which, for the most part,
have been carried through into the peace period and represent
actual earnings. One of the most important factors in regard
to those contingency reserves is the fact that they have not been
deductible for tax purposes during the war period and hence they
are truly appropriated surplus. If some of the money has to be
spent which those reserves refer to, such as, let us say, for
plant relocation or something of that type, that money would be
deductible on the tax returns of the corporations in the future
and would save them a thirty-eight per cent income tax.

One rather interesting question of this sort came up
in the matter of the earnings of the United States Steel
Corporation. I had occasion a year or so ago to speak to a
group of accountants and lawyers on the subject. In analyzing
the United States Steel Company's earnings for a ten-year period,
I indicated that the true earnings were larger than reported
because of the setting up of contingency reserves by the Steel
Corporation. They amounted in this calculation to a total of
$18.60 a share for ten years, or an average of $1.86, and they
added pretty nearly fifty per cent to the earnings of the Steel
Corporation.

I might say, parenthetically, that it was fortunate
the Steel Corporation should have some credit item of that kind,
because its actual record during the war period in terms of
earnings for common stock was otherwise very unsatisfactory. When
you put back the contingency reserves into profits you find that
the average earnings for the ten years 1935-44 were $5.78 per share
For the five years 1941-45 they amounted to about $9 per share,
which would not be called unsatisfactory.

There was some question raised at this point whether
it was proper for the analyst to correct the earnings as reported
by the directors. Some accountants took the stand that if the
directors saw fit to set up this contingency reserve before
stating the earnings, that must mean that in their wisdom and
superior knowledge of the facts those deductions were necessary,
and it was a sort of impiety for the security analyst to lay
violent hands upon the income account as reported. My defense
was that the calculations made by the directors in these contingency reserves were of a remarkably uniform and round-amount
nature each year, and it would be very strange if by a careful
process of calculation the directors would discover that the
Steel Corporation needed exactly $25,000,000 in each successive
year to allow for accruing contingencies. Furthermore, since
the policy with regard to contingencies varies so much from
company to company, the only sound method is to take the
contingency reserves out of the picture for all companies and
make your comparisons exclusive of any charge for contingencies.
But that didn't mean to say -- and this is the point I am

coming to -- that in no case would a company have any use for the contingency reserves. I do not mean to imply that. The main point that I wanted to make was that the contingency reserves were not really related to the earnings of the period in which they were set up, and that they were largely a convenient matter of reducing the earnings in good years and then making the earnings in subsequent years, which may not be so good, seem better.

I want now to carry that through with regard to the earnings of the United States Steel Corporation for the year 1945, because in the year 1945 you had the opposite situation. There they reported earnings of $3.70 a share, which was more or less the same as that for the year before; but in 1945 instead of adding to their contingency reserves before they got the earnings, they subtracted very substantially from the reserves. In fact, they subtracted $38,000,000, or $4.40 a share approximately, So in 1945 the Steel Corporation, if they had not used the device of contingency reserves, would have actually shown a deficit of some size for the common stock. That fact, I think, points up the peculiar problem which the United States Steel Corporation has been facing for a great many years now--its inability to establish a sustained earning power commensurate with the size and position of the corporation.

However, with regard to the Steel Corporation you also have had the strange phenomenon that while their earnings have been relatively poor their financial position has continued to improve. I don't know whether you should say that they are slowly dying of improvement, or that they are slowly growing rich out of adversity. (Laughter.) It's one or the other. For example, last year, although they apparently had such a poor year (particularly when the contingency situation is considered), it turned out that they increased their working capital by no less than about $150,000,000. You may very well ask, "How can you have a very bad year and a situation where you add $150,000,000 to your cash assets?" Well, that's one of the phenomena of the war period, and it will give you some idea of the extraordinary things that have happened in the last couple of years.

The United States Steel Corporation had charged last year their regular depreciation of $77,000,000, which would add to their cash if it were not all spent on new plant. But besides that they charged off all the balance of their war plant expenditures,--known as "emergency plant facilities"--which amounted to the very tidy sum of $157,000,000. Against this charge off they got the benefit of tax credits to a very substantial degree, but not to a complete degree. That was a total charge of $235,000,000, which represented a conversion of fixed assets into cash. Their net expenditure on plant was $24,000,000, so that they actually showed a reduction of their plant account by no less than $211,000,000. In that way you find that although the surplus and reserves decreased $43,000,000 (of which $35,000,000 was in dividends paid) the cash assets increased, as

I said, about $150,000,000. That means, as I see it, that the experience of the Steel Corporation in these recent years cannot be viewed in any definitive way as being basically unsatisfactory or basically satisfactory, but that one would have to reserve judgment on the future position of the corporation.

One additional thing that you will note in the balance sheet: Of these cash funds that I am speaking of, $308,000,000 are not stated by the corporation as being current assets but are put in a fund for future plant expenditures. The Steel Corporation very evidently is under the necessity of making extremely large cash expenditures in order to improve its position in the industry. Here an analyst would have to look forward to the reversal of the situation in the last few years--namely, the conversion of what are now cash assets into fixed assets, in the hope, presumably, that they will be productive of adequate earning power for the corporation.

Now, I don't want to go into the point any further than that, because at this moment I'm only concerned with an interpretation of what has happened and its relationship to specific corporate actions that may take place in the future. I don't want here to go into the field of prophecy with regard to future operating results.

So much for the situation in the United States Steel Corporation as it developed during the war period. Are there any questions?

Related to this particular aspect of the Steel Corporation there are a great many questions that could be asked about its affairs, I am sure.

QUESTION: What is your view on the adequacy or inadequacy of the regular charge-off for depreciation?

MR. GRAHAM: Well, you have every right to raise the point. If you ask my opinion on the subject, it appears that the ordinary depreciation charges of the Steel Corporation have been quite adequate. The $77,000,000 charged in 1945 is a very high figure historically for them. And the amortization of war facilities is something completely separate, as you know. It has given that company, and a great many others, new facilities which do not stand on their books at any cost. In the case of the Steel Corporation it is $299,000,000 worth of new facilities which now they have written down to $1. Are there other questions at this time about that?

The next item that you have to struggle with in analyzing these income accounts is the matter of taxes. Ordinarily the tax problem should not be of any great importance, since it washes itself out over the years when you study any period of earnings. But when you are trying to study the situation more

narrowly with regard to a single year's earnings, then you find
that understanding the tax situation is vital in many cases,
because there are so many different ways in which tax liabilities
can be handled with respect to a single year's operations.

The railroads present the most difficult situation as
a whole in this respect, because their accounting must follow
the requirements of the I.C.C., which were set up around 1911
and which could not anticipate some of the peculiar corporate
developments in subsequent years. Under the I.C.C. accounting,
the rule is that the taxes charged to income for the year should
be the amount actually to be paid to the Government regardless
of the reason for the amounts being large or small. But on the
other hand, profits or losses before taxes on sales of property,
or expenses in connection with bond refundings, and so on, must
go through surplus account. So that you have the typical situation
of a number of railroads in recent years, in which they have
incurred a considerable expense item for premiums paid on
refinancing and discounts incurred and written off on new financing-
the premiums are premiums on redemption of old bonds; the discount
is on the sale of new bonds -- and all that, by I.C.C. regulation,
goes through the surplus account, not into the income account.
But the tax saving thereon (which I don't mind telling you I
believe is the chief reason for many of the refinancing operations
in the last few years) that tax saving appears in the income account.
So by that means you find that the earnings of the railroads have
been overstated in some cases rather substantially.

Let me mention here a contrast,--rather an interesting
one,--between the Gulf Mobile and Ohio, which has to follow
the I.C.C. requirements, and the Twin City Rapid Transit Company,
which can follow its own requirements or those of its Public
Service Commission. In the year 1943 the Gulf Mobile and Ohio
reported earnings of $4.63 a share but in a footnote they say
that their taxes were reduced by the equivalent of $2.18 a share
by reason of loss on property sold and various other surplus
adjustments. We would say, obviously, that the true earnings
from operations were only $2.45 a share, because you cannot
properly increase your earnings as a result of taking losses in
surplus account. On the other hand, the Twin City Rapid Transit
Company in their report for 1944 show that they charge to income
$2,120,000 of taxes, but they credited to surplus $543,000 of
taxes which was the money saved because of debt refunding expense.
That was a proper way, among other proper ways, of dealing with
the situation. They reported in their income account all the
taxes that they would have paid if they did not have the saving
due to their refunding operation; and then in the surplus account
they credit the tax saving against the loss on refunding. Those
points, I think, ought to be pretty clear to you on reflection.

I have raised the question with the Standard Statistics
people and other services as follows: Why don't they restate the
income accounts of railroads so as to reflect the true operations
for the year. If they want to put losses on securities or

property or debt expense in the current picture and take the tax
credit, they can do that. But if they don't want to put these
losses in the current earnings picture, they should not put the
tax savings thereon in the current picture. And the answer, so
far as I can make it out, is that they don't want to meddle with
the I.C.C.'s method of accounting. But it seems to me one of
the chief purposes of a good statistical organization is to do
just that kind of meddling when it is necessary in order to make
the accounting picture fairer or more intelligible.

There are some very interesting further complications
on taxes and I'd like to take a minute or two to give you a
beautiful one. It is the case of Denver and Rio Grande, and
may be compared, let us say, with Northern Pacific, which I intend
to study at greater length for other purposes.

Now, on Denver and Rio Grande, if you looked at the
reports for the last couple of years you would say their earnings
took an awful drop in 1945. They had a loss of $679,000 before
interest charges, and that meant that after interest charges
they lost over $7,000,000. And I suppose that news made some
people pessimistic about the Denver.

The year before they apparently did very well indeed.
They earned $10,588,000 before interest charges, compared with
the deficit in 1945. Now, the striking thing is that when you
do a little analyzing you find that they had a better year in
1945 than they had in 1944, in spite of this difference of
$11,000,000 in the balance reported before interest charges.

I would like to give you a method of analyzing a
railroad's earnings which I believe is rather novel, because I
haven't seen anything like it before -- in fact, I admit I just
invented it today. (Laughter.)

You remember in Comparative Industrial Analysis we
sometimes study the net earnings before taxes and depreciation.
For the net before taxes is a useful item, and the depreciation
may well be treated separately since it is partly arbitrary.
Now I suggest we do the same thing for railroads and find out
what that shows us. Well, here are figures for the Denver
under 1945 and 1944. What we call the operating revenue or
gross was 74.8 million in 1945 as against 70.3 million in 1944.
Then first I'll give you the result of a calculation which
won't appear in your income account,-- namely, the single figure
of net before income taxes and depreciation items. (That is not
maintenance, of course; that's depreciation, money for which cash
has not been spent.) In 1944 this net was $23,220,000 and in 1945
it was $27,721,000. Hence the much poorer reported earnings for
1945 than in 1944 must be due to the fact that Denver charged
off more in 1945 for taxes and depreciation. What are the
figures? Depreciation, et cetera -- and that includes an unusual
item in Denver called "deferred maintenance," not a large amount--

was $16,000,000 this year, against $6,000,000 the year before.
There's $10,000,000 of difference, approximately. Next we have
income taxes, and this is really a first-class surprise. You
would assume that if Denver charged $16,000,000 for depreciation --
and that's mainly amortization of emergency facilities -- that
they would have shown a great benefit in their income taxes. Yet
for 1945 they were able to work out an income tax bill of
$10,576,000, whereas the year before it was only $5,338,000. Thus
in 1945 both depreciation and income taxes were far greater than in
1944.

        Now, you will raise two questions, of course. One is,
did they really do better in 1945 than in 1944? And if they did,
how was it possible for them to appear to have done so very much
worse? The depreciation items you can understand readily. All
the railroads charged off the full amortization of emergency
facilities in 1945, and therefore the charges were higher in 1945
than in 1944. I am not too sure why they all did it, because it
seems to me that in some cases they may not have needed that
amortization for income tax purposes; and if so, it might have
been better for them to have carried it along. But apparently
they all decided to make the full charge-off.

        But the main problem is, how can they have paid so
much for income taxes when their earnings were apparently so bad?
After all, we never heard of a company which had a deficit of
$7,000,000 and had to pay $10,000,000 of income taxes. The
company's report explains it to you in a rather incomplete way.
The first important item is that $7,406,000 of this 1945 tax
represents possible tax deficiencies for previous years. Obviously
this item has nothing at all to do with the current year's
operations. We may hope that there are not really such deficiencies for the past year, but whatever they are they belong to the
past years' operations. Also, the depreciation charge of
$16,000,000 included $5,300,000 applicable to past years, and
consequently the 1945 taxes did not get the benefit of that item,
because that was carried back to past years in some rather
complicated way. The net of the situation in the 1945 operations
include $9,000,000 of amortization and taxes which are applicable
to previous years' operations. If these were eliminated, instead
of having a loss of $7,000,000 for the year's operations after
interest taxes, they would have had a profit of $1,800,000. I
can follow that explanation up to one point which isn't clear.
The taxes that they calculate as belonging to 1945 still amount
to $6,900,000 that they would have to pay. But if their net
earnings after taxes were really 1.8 million, this 1945 tax should
have been about $1,100,000. So there is still a difference of
$5,600,000 not accounted for.

        One thing is quite clear now, to get back to the nub
of the situation: These items are semi-manipulative, you might
say. They have very little to do with the actual operating
results of the Denver. Hence if you want to use the 1945 results

in an evaluation of the system's earning power, you obviously
must give your primary attention to the $27,700,000 earned
before taxes and depreciation, as compared with the $23,440,000
in 1944.

In 1946, of course, the Denver is not doing well. Very
few roads are doing well. But the Denver is managing to earn
money now against losses previously, but they are charging no
income tax this year whereas last year they charged this enormous
amount. Are there any questions about the peculiar elements
of the Denver picture?

QUESTION: It might help in obtaining higher rates.

MR. GRAHAM: Well, the I.C.C. have pretty good
accountants, and my guess is that they are going to look at the
balance before taxes and depreciation more intently than at the
loss after bond interest. The thing that a Denver bondholder
should hope for is that the income taxes were really overstated
in 1945 and that perhaps the Denver won't have to pay those
items, but has merely set up reserves for them on some theoretical
basis. Are there any other questions?

QUESTION: Might they not justify their accounting
on the basis that it created public opinion or helped to create
public opinion which would be favorable?

MR. GRAHAM: Well, I really wouldn't want to express
an opinion. I think if the Denver were the only railroad in the
country, or if it were a really important road, there might be
something in it. I don't believe their figures received much
public attention because it is a receivership road. Are there
any other questions?

Now, by way of contrast we might take the figures of
the Northern Pacific for the years 1945 and 1944, which do not
involve extraordinary problems of this kind but do involve similar
items. In 1944 Northern Pacific showed earnings of $50 million
before amortization and income tax, and in 1945 they showed
earnings of $41.4, which was a decrease of a fair amount. The
figures for amortization were $12,600,000 in 1944, and $35,500,000
in 1945, which is an enormous figure for the Northern Pacific,
and I think it has great significance. But their income-tax
figures were much more normal. They had a charge of $17.8
million in 1944, and they got a credit of eight million dollars
in 1945 as a result of all this amortization. So that the two
items combined were not very different in the two years. They
were $30.5 million in 1944 and $27.5 million in 1945--which of
course would not call for the kind of comment we made in the Denver
case.

But there is one further item to call your attention to,
and that is that the Northern Pacific had surplus adjustments of
about $7,600,000 in 1945, mainly for refinancing expense. Thus

they got the benefit of a tax credit there, which I assume was in the sum of about $3,000,000. Hence if you want to make a careful analysis of the Northern Pacific situation for that year you would have to assume that their true earnings were about $3,000,000, or a dollar a share less than reported for the year 1945. There are other more interesting elements in the Northern Pacific that I would like to talk about in my next lecture.

I have about ten minutes left, and I think I would like to go on to this question of the significance of amortization of war facilities which has already been raised once or twice this afternoon. One interesting place to start with is the aircraft companies that I mentioned to you earlier. Here, for example, is a quick skeleton view of Curtiss Wright: Working capital which we call NCA, or net current assets, in 1940 was $13,800,000. Other assets, that's mainly plant of course, were $32,400,000, giving you $46,200,000 of equity for your stock issues We'll put down here floor space owned, 2,672,000 square feet in 1941. (I haven't got it for 1940.)

Now, at the end of 1945 we have this situation: The net current assets are $138,200,000, which is almost exactly ten times what they were five years before; the other assets, mainly plant, are only $10,900,000, giving a total of $149,100,000; the floor space owned is 3,093,000 square feet. In addition, they had a great deal of leased floor space and also Government-owned floor space, the significance of which I am not prepared to comment on. But what you find has happened in the Curtiss Wright case is that they have undoubtedly enlarged their facilities substantially, and at the same time they have written down their plant account to a very small figure. Interestingly enough, I think the chief item in their plant account is facilities held for sale. It's a bit ironical that of this $10.9 million, six million dollars are in real estate, machinery and equipment held for sale or disposal, and that the operating facilities, which are really the three million square feet, are carried at only $4,000,000 in that company.

In the case of United Aircraft, you have somewhat the same situation--in some respects more extreme. In five years the working capital went up from $13,000,000 to $85,000,000 after deducting their preferred stock, as equivalent to a current liability. Their plant facilities went down from $25,600,000 to $5,800,000-- only about twenty per cent of what they were. Undoubtedly they are more valuable now than six years ago.

Therefore, as was suggested, there probably is a true element of hidden earnings in the balance sheet situation, due to these amortization practices. These companies have not only increased their working capital but they probably have increased the true value of their plant account substantially. Certainly they did not decrease it, and therefore from the standpoint of a private owner of the business he can be pretty sure that he has

not only the great increase in working capital but at least as
much as he had before in plant account. Are there any questions
about that?

Now, the Northern Pacific has an interesting similar
situation in regard to their plant account, consisting of road
and equipment. The Northern Pacific Company in the four years
ending with 1940 had a typical picture: namely, they spent about
$10,000,000 on road and equipment, depreciated about $4,000,000,
and increased their fixed assets by $6,000,000. That was
representative pre-war practice.

In the war the situation is completely different. They
spent $23,000,000 on road, $33,007,000 on equipment, or a total
of $56.7 million. They charged off fifty-nine million for
amortization in those five years. Thus they decreased their
plant account by two million dollars, although they added these
very important facilities to the road. I am not prepared to say
whether Northern Pacific is thoroughly representative of all the
railroads, or whether it is a somewhat extreme case. My
impression is that it is not very different from the typical
railroad of its size. And so you have to take into account in
your analysis of the railroad picture that these roads have
added greatly to their physical facilities without adding to
the plant account on their books--and of course without incurring
any debt in relation thereto. As a matter of fact, the railroads
have done just the opposite and have decreased their debt very
greatly.

I would like to point out with regard to the position
of the railroads over the years that the increase in the working
capital of the railroads is the most impressive item to be found
in the study of working capital changes that has been put out
by the Securities and Exchange Commission recently. The
percentage increase of the railroads was much greater than that
of industrials as a whole, and also of your public utilities.
You might almost say that the financial position of the railroads
has been practically revolutionized during the war. As you know
in addition to increasing their cash assets enormously, the
railroads have made very great reductions in the principal amount
of their debt and also have effected great reductions in some
cases in the average interest charges on their debt. An analyst
with something of a memory would say that World War II is very
different (in relation to the financial impact) than World War I
in that very respect. What happened in World War I was that the
typical large industrial that had been in a speculative and
fairly weak position emerged from that war greatly strengthened
financially. In World War II the chief financial improvement
is to be found in the position of the railroads. And I believe
that it is a matter of more significance than we are likely
to give it. I say that because of the pronounced pessimism
with regard to the future of the railroads at this time due to
their difficulties in wage costs and their rate struggle. But

getting back again to the safe haven of historical experience
(which doesn't carry any guarantees to future continuance), the
thing that has hurt the railroads as a whole, and the thing that
has hurt the individual railroad, has been their financial
position. In the past they have always been able to deal with
their operating expenses one way or the other--by greater
efficiency or higher rates. The thing that they haven't been
able to deal with was their debt. That point may have considerable
significance for the future of our carriers.

           I believe this is a good moment to close this lecture.
We will go on ahead to the next one with further information
on analysis of past results.

Lecture No. 3   October 22, 1946

CURRENT PROBLEMS IN SECURITY ANALYSIS

By
Benjamin Graham
****

We intend to go on with the subject matter of the last
two lectures, which was consideration of special factors that
have entered ito income account and balance-sheet analysis in
the last few years of wartime and postwartime conditions.

I would like to start with one or two references to
material that has come up in the last couple of weeks which is
indicative of the type of thing that the security analyst will
have to deal with recurrently.

A few days ago the Republic Aviation Company published
its June 30, 1946, balance sheet and income account, and showed
earnings of $6000, or one cent a share in that first half. But
if you examine the balance sheet you would see that the working
capital decreased from $10,035,000 at the end of 1945, to
$7,565,000 six months later. That was a loss of about twenty-five
per cent. Also the book value of the stock decreased from
$12.70 to $10.04, which was a loss of some 20%. This obviously
should call for a further study of what happened in that six-month
period.

The earnings of one cent a share are certainly not
indicative of the true results; and when you trace the thing
through you will find that there were two matters that had a
bearing on the company's position at the end of the period. One
was that they transferred $486,000 from balance sheet reserves
to the credit of income; that was on the order of fifty cents a
share. But the other and more important fact is that they paid
out $1,500,000--or $1.60 per share--for 1944 renegotiation
settlement, which sum was also charged to reserve account. There
you see an example of what we were discussing two weeks ago--the
divergent treatment of renegotiation items.

Republic did not make provision for its full renegotiation obligations as a current liability, but only in the
general reserves. When it was necessary for that company actually
to settle with the Government these reserves became actual
liabilities in the amount of a million and a half for renegotiation
as well as in the amount of half a million dollars for other
purposes. Those are important items in quantity, in the case of
a company like Republic; and they reduced the working capital by
a substantial amount.

Now, if you would like to look at the corresponding report of United Aircraft, you will see that a somewhat similar situation developed; that is to say, that they showed earnings of ninety-two cents a share, all of which were made possible by the fact that they used credit of a million six from their contingency reserves and also that they took a tax credit of seven million dollars for that period. But the effect in the case of United Aircraft was not at all as important because their working capital shrank only one per cent during that period as compared with about twenty-four per cent for Republic, and the net asset value fell only about fifteen cents a share.

You see, therefore, that the attitude of the analyst on these matters must be guided very much by the question of how important the specific development is for the company in regard to its own position and the amounts involved, and not by the general question whether you are or are not using up reserves and tax credits, and so forth.

Now, are there any questions about that reference to the Republic situation and the United Aircraft situation? It is somewhat anomalous that Republic was one of the few aircraft companies that sold very much above its tangible asset value at the beginning of this year. As a matter of fact, I think it is still selling above its tangible asset value, although it apparently was more vulnerable to loss of value as a result of postwar accounting developments than other aircraft companies. Whether that price of Republic reflects primarily confidence of the security public in the future operations of Republic as compared with those of other companies, or whether it represents in part an overappraisal of what they accomplished in the past, is a matter for you to decide. I am just stating the facts as I see them; that is, the facts in relation to the past operations. Are there any questions about the Republic analysis?

Now, there is one other item that came to my attention a few days ago which has a bearing on war accounting and that is a reference to what is known as "Lifo," which means last in, first out. I presume most of you are familiar with that accounting principle. It has had a rather important effect upon the balance-sheet figures of some corporations, but not quite so important on their income accounts.

Lifo is an accounting method, permitted by new income-tax regulations beginning about 1942, under which instead of considering that the first purchased merchandise is sold or used up in manufacture, the corporation is permitted to assume that the last purchased merchandise is sold or used up. As a result, the inventory is kept down during a period of rising prices because it is not necessary to mark up the value of the quantities of inventory owned at the time that the rising prices began. The result of using that method is (a) to reduce inventory values below market values, and in some cases by a very considerable amount; (b) to reduce accordingly the reported profits; and (c) and most important, perhaps, to reduce the amount of taxes which have to be paid.

What you have, then, in the balance sheets is either an understatement of the true value of the inventory, if you want to consider it that; or a cushion to absorb declines in inventory values without effecting a cash loss if you wish more conservatively to consider Lifo that way.

In the case of the Federated Department Stores, their report which appeared a few days ago gives some details on Lifo, which they find necessary to do because of a tax problem facing them. That company showed that since 1942 they had the benefit of a reduction in inventory and taxable profit of $3,875,000 by using Lifo instead of using the usual fist-in, first-out method. That enabled them to reduce their taxes by $2,590,000; and it reduced their profits after taxes for the five and a half years by roughly $1,150,000.

The difficulty that they refer to is the fact that in department stores it is practically impossible to identify the items that are sold in relation to just when they were bought. Consequently the department stores have tried to use something called an "index of retail price changes" to determine what would be the effect of Lifo on their accounting. And they now are in a controversy with the Treasury because the Treasury says that the Lifo section does not permit the use of estimates by means of an index as to what last-in, first-out means, and therefore they must go back to their old method of first-in, first-out.

The significance of Lifo is interesting, when you reflect upon it, because it is very similar to the wartime amortization of plant facilities which we discussed two weeks ago. There, you recall, the companies had the opportunity to write down their fixed assets, which were recently acquired, to zero, and to get the benefit of tax credits, the effect of which, however, was to reduce their earnings somewhat. You have exactly the same effect here in Lifo. You write down your inventory, save a great deal of money in taxes, but reduce your apparent earnings somewhat.

I think that for the analyst the significant thing is that the Lifo method is one of the additional conservative elements that have come into corporate accounting in the last five or six years. These will probably buttress corporations against losses that might otherwise take place during a depression; and I think we ought to recognize that factor as on the plus side in security values.

In very few reports do you have any information as to the exact amount involved in Lifo, but in the case of the Federated Department Stores you have the advantage of having the whole picture spread before you. Are there any questions about that?

STUDENT: I suppose you have to be consistent when you start taking last items; you can't jump back to first, if that should be more convenient.

MR. GRAHAM: No, my understanding is that you can change that accounting method only by permission of the Treasury Department. That is a rule that applies to a number of other optional ways of dealing with accounting. Davenport?

STUDENT: Wouldn't you mention that whereas that method results in reducing the earnings when prices are rising, it results also in increasing the earnings when prices are declining?

MR. GRAHAM: Yes. I'm glad you raised that point. It would be the natural effect of having introduced a conservative factor into your balance sheet. Since you carry your inventory at a lower price than you otherwise would, you either reduce your losses, if there would have been losses, or you increase your profits when you sell them out, as compared with the other basis. As a matter of fact, you gain also in dollars because the tax that was saved during the war period by Lifo was at a very high rate and the tax that you ultimately pay when you realize those profits again will be at a lower rate. And that's an important net gain over the years. Are there any other questions about Lifo?

Now, I'd like to go on to a more elaborate discussion by which we can perhaps terminate this part of our course, a discussion of the influence of the war period on the position of a company. I have taken as an example the Northern Pacific Railway, which I've already mentioned in connection with their amortization write-offs.

Northern Pacific is interesting because its picture involves not only the general question of the effect of the war period on railroads, but a number of special situations that should interest the analyst and which apply to this company more or less uniquely.

If you were asked to analyze Northern Pacific you might start off in a conventional way and say that this company at recent low prices did not show the stockholder any advantage out of the war period because during the years 1936-40 its market price averaged 16-1/2, and recently at the low it also sold at 16-1/2. Thus the stockholder is apparently back where he started, in spite of the war earnings.

During the period 1936-1940 the reported results averaged a very small deficit, whereas during the period 1941-45 they averaged $6.20 a share. Since they paid only a dollar annual dividend, in four of the years, they added $27 a share to their surplus in that five years. None of that is reflected in the current market price.

If you want to trace the twenty-seven dollars through, you will see that about two-thirds of it is in the form of a debt decrease and the other third in the form of an increase in their working capital.

I have previously mentioned the fact that they added about $57,000,000 -- that's roughly $25 a share -- to their road and equipment account, all of which had been written off during the period. That may be an added element of strength or value to the road, but it does not appear in the balance sheet or in the reported earnings.

If you carry the analysis further you would say that they have succeeded during this period in cutting down their fixed charges considerably. In 1940 they were $15,100,000, and in 1946 they are about $10,600,000, or a reduction of thirty per cent. That is considerably more than the percentage reduction in principal amount of debt, and, of course, reflects refundings at lower interest charges.

Then, finally, when you look at 1946 earnings you would see that for eight months the company reported earnings of seventy-four cents as against $3.60 in 1945. And when you completed that story I think you would have a somewhat mixed conclusion as to what it means for the investor. For you would say that here is a company that had done a great deal to improve its situation in five years, and the market doesn't reflect that at all. But on the other hand it is not at all clear that it should reflect it, because now in 1946 the company seems to be back pretty much where it was pre-war, with no substantial earnings.

That is what I would call a conventional current analysis of Northern Pacific, but I think it is quite superficial. There is a good deal more to that situation.

When you look a little more closely at Northern Pacific you will find that the main factor affecting this company, that does not affect other companies, is its large interest in an affiliated railroad which is not shown in its income account, except in the form of dividends. Northern Pacific owns 48-1/2% of the Burlington, or C.B. & Q. Now, the Burlington is rather paradoxically bigger and a much better railroad than the Northern Pacific. You have thus a rather unusual situation, in which the chief interest perhaps of the stockholders of the Northern Pacific does not appear except in a very indirect and incomplete way in its own reports.

In addition to that interest in the Burlington the Northern Pacific owns fifty per cent of a rather substantial railroad system called the Spokane-Portland-Seattle, which before

the war had no earning power but which during the war had quite
substantial earnings. In addition to that, the Northern Pacific
has a land department which has been productive of rather substantial income over the years. This does not appear in the income
account but the proceeds or profits are credited to surplus
directly. When you start taking account of these additional
interests of the Northern Pacific you find that the picture is
quite different than it appeared in the first analysis.

In the period 1936-1940 there would be no substantial
change, because the Burlington paid out practically all that it
earned in that period. Instead of having a small loss on the
stock you would have an equally minor profit of about twelve
cents a share.

But when you take the war period 1941-1945, you find
that to the $6.20 average shown by Northern Pacific there is to
be added $3.80 per share in undistributed profits of Burlington;
about 86 cents per share representing the earnings of S.P.&S.;
and about 60 cents per share representing the land department--
giving you a total of $11.46, which is pretty nearly twice the
figures actually reported. These are average earnings per year
for five years. Thus you find that there is what used to be called
a "hidden equity" of about twenty-six dollars a share additional
in those five years, making a total of about fifty-three dollars
that has gone back into the stockholders' account for Northern
Pacific as compared with the pre-war period.

If you look at the Burlington you will see that its
own undistributed profits show up in a considerable reduction in
funded debt, a reduction of thirty-six per cent in fixed charges,
and a considerable increase in working capital. You would find
that the earnings of the Spokane railroad show up in the form of
$20,000,000 additional working capital, of which $10,000,000
inures to the Northern Pacific.

When you come to the period of the first eight months
of 1946, you find that instead of having earnings only seventy-four
cents a share, the earnings, including the Burlington equity,
are $2.80 a share for the eight months. The indications are that
they will earn about five dollars a share for the full year,
including the Burlington equity.

That, of course, is a very different picture from the
rather negligible earnings which they reported for the first
eight months. You have also some figures that have been put in
the record with the I.C.C. in connection with the rate-increase
application. These show that if they get a ten per cent further
increase, (which is more or less the figure that Wall Street is
expecting or hoping for,) they might earn about $4 per share in
1947 on their own income account and perhaps $8 a share, including
their equity in the Burlington.

Now, those are very substantial figures in relation to the current market price. They indicate the importance of looking at the railroad on the consolidated basis rather than on the basis of the earnings as they were reported.

An interesting further study of Northern Pacific could be carried on by comparing it with some other road. This would give you some idea of its relative position and its attractiveness. I would suggest therefore that we devote a little time to a comparison between Northern Pacific and Southern Pacific. There is a relationship in names there that would make the comparison a natural one.

You might suggest that the comparison should be made with Great Northern, because Northern Pacific and Great Northern have always been grouped together in general railroad analysis, and you know that each of them owns approximately half of the Burlington. However, the Great Northern has managed to put itself into a stronger capital structure position than Northern Pacific, partly through the conversion of bonds into stock. The Great Northern belongs somewhat more in the investment category. On the other hand, as we shall see, Southern Pacific is about in the same general financial situation as Northern Pacific with respect to stock and bond capitalization structure. That is a fundamental basis of allocating roads to classes for comparison. As you know, Northern Pacific sells now about 19, and Southern Pacific about 42. There you have a ratio of somewhat more than two to one. If we go back to the superficial earnings, you would see that before the war Southern Pacific averaged $1.27 per share for five years, 1936 to 1940, while Northern Pacific had a very small deficit. In the five years 1941 to 1945 Southern Pacific showed $12.90, against $6.20 for Northern Pacific, which is about our ratio of two to one; and in eight months of 1946, Southern Pacific shows $3.86 against $.74 for Northern Pacific, which is much better than a two to one ratio.

STUDENT: Does Northern Pacific use its carry-back in the first eight months the way Southern Pacific did?

MR. GRAHAM: That's a point that I shall come to. We have just spoken now about the figures as they appear in the reported earnings picture per share. Now we make two adjustments for that, one of them being the question of taxes which has just been raised. You find when you study the Southern Pacific figures that in 1946 they have had a tax credit of about $19,000,000, which is more than the earnings reported for that period. Northern Pacific had a small tax payment of its own and fairly substantial taxes for Burlington; so that they do not use any tax credit but, on the contrary, pay full taxes on their earnings.

If you compare the situation, putting in Northern Pacific's Burlington interest, you would find that while the 1936-1940 figures remain about the same, for the war period

Northern Pacific's earnings rise to $11.46, as compared with
$12.90 for Southern Pacific,--very nearly the same. For the
eight months of 1946, Northern Pacific's earnings before taxes,
without allowances for income tax debit or credit, would be $4.60,
while those of Southern Pacific would be a deficit of $1.20.

In a peculiar way, therefore, the situation seems to
have been reversed. Whereas before the war Northern Pacific
apparently tended toward a deficit and Southern Pacific toward
moderate earnings, we now find that under 1946 conditions Southern
Pacific seems to be tending toward a deficit and Northern Pacific
toward fairly good earnings.

That analysis, of course, calls for much further
probing into the situation. You have to ask yourself why it is
that you get these diverse developments in the different periods
that we are studying. What you find is that Southern Pacific in
1946 has apparently lost control over its expense ratio more
seriously than has happened to Northern Pacific and to Burlington.
As a matter of fact, the Burlington has been doing a very nice
job of maintaining its net earnings even under the unfavorable
wage and rate situation which we have had in 1946.

Northern Pacific itself has not done so well, but it
has done better than Southern Pacific; and the combination shows
up very much better. As you study the figures more carefully,
you find that an advantage which Southern Pacific seemed to have
developed in its operating ratio during the pre-war and early
war years has now seemed to have reversed itself or disappeared;
and the advantage, is now in the Northern railroads.

If you study the Southern Pacific figures over a period
of time, you will see that of course the Southern Pacific
derived great advantages out of the war. It increased its
surplus and its working capital considerably; it decreased its
debt a great deal, and cut its fixed charges by about twenty
per cent. That figure is not quite as good as the decrease
shown by the Northern Pacific-Burlington combination.

Another factor that should get attention from the
security analyst in studying these railroads is the question of
rentals and hire of equipment. In the ordinary way in which
fixed charges are stated in the manuals, and elsewhere, you would
get the impression that the coverage of fixed charges for
Southern Pacific is quite a good deal better than that of
Northern Pacific--or was, let us say, up to this year. Actually
that is not the case if you consider rentals and hire of
equipment, (with payments and receipts), as part of your over-all
fixed charge situation.

Those of you who have studied our text on Security
Analysis will recall our reference to the "net deductions
method" in which you replace fixed charges by a figure

representing the difference between the net after taxes and the balance for stock.

On that basis you will find that Northern Pacific has a considerable advantage, because it has regularly received sub- stantial credits from hire of equipment and joint facilities. In 1945 these were $4,346,000. But Southern Pacific has made very heavy payments for the same purpose; in 1945 they were $24,600,000.

If you restate your fixed charge coverage by allowing for the equipment and joint facility rental payments and also put in Northern Pacific figures its share of the Burlington, you will find this situation is also true for the eight months of 1946. Southern Pacific's net deductions were $24,300,000 in eight months, which was about 7-1/2 per cent of gross, the latter being around $320,000,000.

Northern Pacific's net deductions were $9,180,000 on gross of $143,000,000. This is on a pro-rata consolidated basis, which includes 48-1/2% of Burlington. Thus you would find that the ratio is on the order of six and a half per cent of gross. The relationship to net is better for Northern Pacific than for Southern Pacific, because Northern Pacific's operating ratio is less.

These are factors which I am calling to your attention because they do not enter generally into the analytical presenta- tion of a railroad's showing. And you find that when you allow for these factors you get a very considerable difference in the picture than when you started with the figures that were first available.

An interesting question to ask is why the showing of Northern Pacific has apparently improved considerably from 1941 as against Southern Pacific, whereas that of Southern Pacific showed the improvement between 1937 and 1941. I don't want to go into the details of that matter because they are rather complicated; but you will find them in an analysis of the operating ratios to which I referred and which are worked out for you in the Standard Statistics description of both systems.

Does this analysis indicate the Northern Pacific is undervalued in relation to Southern Pacific at the present time? In answering that question we find ourselves confronted with a number of considerations. One of them, of course, is that very possibly Southern Pacific sells too high in relation to Northern Pacific because investors don't appreciate the true position of Northern Pacific, including the Burlington interest and the other factors.

The next question, however, is a somewhat different one. One very good reason why Southern Pacific sells so much higher than Northern Pacific is because it is paying dividends at the rate

of $4 and Northern Pacific is paying dividends at the rate of $1.
It is obvious that such a disparity in dividend policies would
have a substantial effect on market prices.

A question that we shall have to consider from time to
time in the future is how valid is the dividend rate as a
determinant of proper market prices.   That it actually has a great
effect on market price cannot be denied--certainly in the field
of securities that are bought by investors.

Two years ago, when we were giving a course here on
appraisal of stocks, we had occasion to compare Reading and
Pennsylvania.   There we found that Reading and Pennsylvania made
practically the same showing with regard to earnings and financial
strength.   But Reading was satisfied to pay a dollar to its stockholders, while Pennsylvania was paying about two dollars and a
half.   The result was that you had prices averaging $20 for
Pennsylvania in 1945, against $24 for Reading.   Before that time,
I think, the ratio of prices was about two to one, although the
ratio of earnings was about the same.

I have also had occasion recently to see rather start-
ling evidence of the effect of dividend policy on prices in a
number of the insurance companies.   If you take two companies like
New Amsterdam Casualty Company and the United States Fidelity &
Guaranty, you would find that these companies are almost identical
in every respect, in the character of their business and their
assets, except that one of them has twice the amount of stock
and twice the assets and business.   The earnings per share are
about the same.   But United States Fidelity pays $2 and New
Amsterdam Casualty $1, and so you have a relationship in price of
$42 for one and $26 for the other.

There is no doubt, therefore, that the dividend rates of
Southern Pacific and Northern Pacific are sufficient to explain
the market relationship, even by themselves, without reference to
any other questions that the analyst might ask himself.

We must consider later -- but I don't think we shall do
it now -- whether the analyst can take advantage of the fact that
two companies would be worth, say, approximately the same amount
from every standpoint other than dividends, and sell at considerable difference because of dividend policy.   The question that
would come up is whether you can expect in the normal course of
events that the dividend policy will adjust itself to the earnings
and that therefore eventually the market price will adjust itself
to the earnings and will not be determined by an arbitrary
dividend policy.   That is a very difficult question to reach a
conclusion about, and I prefer to talk about it at some other time.

There is a final question with regard to the explanation
of the relative prices of Northern Pacific and Southern Pacific,
and that is the question of future influences on earnings.   Would

you say that the prices of these two roads reflect some careful
appraisal by people who know what the future is likely to bring
for one railroad as compared with the other? My personal opinion
is that such is not the case. In fact, it seems to me very
improbable that the market prices can reflect an estimate of
future conditions carefully arrived at, when it is perfectly
evident they don't reflect any real knowledge of what the past
conditions have been, which are open to those who wish to study
them with care. While it is true that they may reflect some
impressions about what the future may have in store for one railroad as against the other, I am quite convinced in my own mind
that the prices in the market do not reflect any considerable
knowledge, of inherent factors which lead to a view as to the
future.

STUDENT: One of the appraisals that I hear is that
since Southern Pacific is so largely in the Southwest, Texas, in
a territory that is growing much more rapidly than the Northwest
territory, that some rail analysts are strong in their preference
for Southern Pacific on that basis over Northern Pacific.

MR. GRAHAM: There is an undoubted impression that the
future of the Southwest territory is better than that of the
Northwest territory. You have some justification for that in the
most recent figures of development of gross earnings. I would
like to give some figures on that which would show how these
companies have developed over the last ten years in relation to
volume.

In 1937 the gross of Northern Pacific, plus forty-eight
per cent of Burlington, was $113,500,000, and Southern Pacific
was $225,000,000. That is almost exactly two to one.

In 1941, Southern Pacific showed a slight increase in
the ratio--$147.3 for Northern Pacific versus $297.8 for Southern
Pacific. By 1944 Southern Pacific had drawn quite a bit ahead
of the Northern Pacific combination. In 1944 it was $254,000,000
for Northern Pacific and $597,000,000 for Southern Pacific. And
that advantage has persisted up to 1946 for the first eight months.

The question that one would raise about those figures
is the extent to which they have reflected the impact of war
conditions since 1941, and whether or not they would be expected
to continue in the future. Frankly, I don't know what the answer
is. Furthermore, I don't know how important such changes with
regard to gross earnings may be in the final earning power of the
railroads.

One of the anomalous things -- and this is very
extraordinary -- that you find in your analysis is the following:
In 1937 the net earnings of Northern Pacific after taxes were
15 million on a gross of $133,400,000. (that is railway operating
income.) Those of Southern Pacific were 34 million one on a gross

of $225,000,000. In other words, Southern Pacific showed up quite
a bit better in net than it did in gross; it had a better than
two to one ratio as against Northern Pacific.

In the first eight months of 1946 the net earnings of
Northern Pacific before income taxes and depreciation, were
$27,700,000, or pretty nearly twenty per cent of its gross; and
those of Southern Pacific were only $29,500,000, which was just
about nine per cent of its gross. Although Southern Pacific
showed a very considerable improvement in its gross earnings as
against Northern Pacific, its net earnings before taxes, depreciation charges, and interest charges were very much poorer proportionatly. The explanation of that, as I said before, is found
in the details of its transportation and maintenance expenditures,
which apparently have grown very much more rapidly for Southern
Pacific than they have for Northern Pacific-Burlington.

The question that was asked about the general future
prospects of one territory as compared with another is certainly
very relevant to analysis of railroad securities. Yet I must
say that I have found in my own work that you can count very much
more dependably upon differences of value which can be established
from the earnings and expense picture than you can on those which
seem to be inherent in the possibilities of the different terri-
tories. Are there any other questions about that factor? It is
one that I didn't intend to go into in too much detail, because
we haven't yet reached the stage where we want to talk about
estimates of earning power based upon future prospects. We are
still in the stage of analyzing past results. But are there any
other factors in that matter?

STUDENT: Possibly the reason for the higher maintenance
charge of the Southern Pacific is that it has a poor roadbed,
very poor equipment. Right on that subject one of the hidden flies
in the ointment in the railroad picture is that they weren't able
to replace equipment during the war period, and although they
scaled down their debt they will be obliged to incur very heavy
debt when they improve their roadbed, when they improve their
rolling stock, when they put in radio control, and so on. As a
matter of fact, along with that thought there is considerable talk
now of having plastic ties to replace wooden ties in order to
eliminate the very heavy labor charge of replacements, and there
has been so much publicity given to the tremendous reduction in
railroad debt that I'm wondering how much of that is an illusion,
is just a temporary reduction because more debt will have to be
piled on when much needed capital improvement occurs.

MR. GRAHAM: Well, the general statement about the
incurring of debt for capital improvements is--(or at least you
get it, from the railroad offices)--that those things are authorized
on the basis of expected budgetary savings, which presumably will
take care of the additional interest charges with a very large
margin.

STUDENT: The point I am making, sir, is that they have been wearing out their equipment, and that invisible loss that has been occurring hasn't reflected itself in the income statement.

MR. GRAHAM: Well, let's see. When you are speaking of equipment, if you mean the actual freight cars and locomotives--

STUDENT: Roadbed too.

MR. GRAHAM: Well, the roadbed is a different thing, of course. It's much easier to talk about the freight cars and the locomotives, because you have more information as to the exact status of those things.

The railroads, of course, will do a great deal of equipment financing in the next ten years. And that happens to be a type of financing that is relatively inexpensive. But nevertheless it will add, to their total funded debt. You must remember that on the basis that you now have of railroad accounting, you have charges for depreciation both of roadway and equipment, and the charges are now running at a pretty important rate. For example, in the case of the Northern Pacific-Burlington, the depreciation charge for eight months was $7,200,000; that's at the rate of about $10,800,000 for depreciation, on their combination earnings of about $200,000,000, or over five per cent.

Those depreciative charges are available for additional equipment, purchases, and debt payments. With regard to ties, which you mentioned, that is quite a different story. It is inconceivable to me that any railroad is going to rip up its present ties and replace them by plastic ties.

STUDENT: There has been considerable talk of that in responsible railroad quarters.

MR. GRAHAM: I would consider that almost incredible. I should think when the time came for them to replace their ties, as they do all the time, they might very well put a plastic tie instead of a creosoted tie. But that would be part of the general tie replacement program which they carry on all the time. Whether they have failed to replace the appropriate quantity of ties in the last five years or so, I don't know. I'm inclined to think that they have failed to do so, because they have had difficulties in getting labor and materials. And there probably is a certain amount of deferred maintenance in the railroads which you would have to allow for.

The Denver and Rio Grande Western, as I mentioned two weeks ago, is one of the few railroads which actually set up a reserve for deferred maintenance, but the amount has not been very large. It has been really rather unimportant in amount, and if that represented the full amount of the deferred maintenance it wouldn't be a matter of any special importance in that railroad or others.

Of course, this doesn't have any particular bearing on the discussion of the relative position of Northern Pacific and Southern Pacific. It bears rather on the position of all the railroads as a whole.

STUDENT: The point I was making there was that anyone who has traveled on the Southern Pacific knows that during the war they had flat wheels, you bumped around all night, and so forth.

MR. GRAHAM: I see. Well I knew I made a trip on it only last March and I didn't care for it too much. But the earnings picture of the Southern Pacific is really a very extraordinary one in relation to the dropping off of their railway operating income in the first eight months of this year as compared with a year ago. As a matter of fact, on 324 million of gross they had only $5,700,000 of net railway operating income before tax credit; and that, of course, is an extraordinarily small figure. Those who are studying the future of that railroad, and others such as Northern Pacific, would have to start today with these very high operating ratios and try to figure out why it is that the earnings have been so badly affected.

Before we close I want to talk about another point that I didn't mention, as follows: You recall I said in the case of Northern Pacific you could only get appropriate picture of the company showing by including its interest in the Burlington, and for that matter also in the Spokane-Seattle-Portland Railroad. You might very well have asked, Why shouldn't the same thing be done for other railroads, as for example Southern Pacific? And the answer is that you can do it, but it isn't worthwhile. That's the important thing.

In the Southern Pacific report you have twelve subsidiary railroads which, if you want to take the trouble to, you could include in the Southern Pacific showing. But when you have done that for eleven of them you have added so little to the Southern Pacific's earnings,--an amount of, say, thirty cents a share or less,--that it isn't worth going to that trouble.

There is one exception there, and that is the St. Louis Southwestern, which had large earnings. The Southern Pacific has a very substantial stock interest in the St. Louis Southwestern, which is in trusteeship. Unfortunately, under the reorganization plan the stock interest is being wiped out; hence it would not be appropriate to include in the Southern Pacific any equity in the St. Louis Southwestern because of its stock interest. In the other eleven subsidiary railroads the matter is not important.

Perhaps we'll start next week with some more questions on this Northern Pacific matter, but our time is up now.

Lecture No. 4   November 19, 1946

CURRENT PROBLEMS IN SECURITY ANALYSIS

By
Benjamin Graham
****

I find one of the students presents me with a question
which I shall be glad to answer for his benefit and for the
benefit of the class. He quotes a statement made in "Security
Analysis," page 691, which says, "Judging from observations made
over a number of years, it would seem that investment in apparently undervalued common stocks can be carried on with a fair
degree of over-all success, provided average alertness and good
judgment are used in passing on the future prospect question,
and provided also that commitments are avoided at the times when
the general market is statistically too high."

That is our statement, and his question is: "that, after
reading the article in the Financial Chronicle which we distributed, one reaches the conclusion that you consider 185 for the
Dow-Jones Average statistically very high. In general, above
what Dow-Jones Average price would you consider it high and
between what ranges would you consider it normal?"

That certainly is a very direct and leading question,
but I would like to start with a correction. If I recall the
article of October, 1945, in the Financial Chronicle, in which
we discussed the then level of stock prices, it was not our
conclusion that the level of one-eight-five was statistically
very high. The conclusion, was that it was <u>historically</u> very
high. That is quite a difference. We pointed out that in the
past the market had not been able to go beyond that level without
getting into dangerous territory.

As far as the statistical discussion was concerned, I
think we found that 185 or thereabouts would appear to be a normal
valuation for the Dow-Jones average as of last year, and that
on a statistical basis there was no particular reason to be
afraid of the stock market there. Our point was, though, that
historically there was reason to be afraid of it, and we were
inclined to advise caution for that reason. As near as we are
able to determine a central value for the Dow-Jones industrials,
we are inclined to believe that somewhere around the present level
or a little bit higher perhaps might be a central level in the
future. The figure we gave provisionally in that article was
178 as so-called "appraisal value." For that reason there would
be no special cautionary factor in the current general level,

working against the purchase of under-valued securities. The only caution we would want to add to that is this: If by any chance you are still going through the usual alternations of bull markets and bear markets,--which is by no means unlikely--then there is no particular reason to believe that when the market has receded to about its average value it would necessarily have stopped going down. Experience in former markets indicates that just as they are too high in bull markets, they get too low in bear markets. If we are going through a similar experience now, the historical analogies would point to lower prices simply because in bear markets securities sell for less than they are worth, just as they sell for more than they are worth in bull markets. Whether that means that a person should avoid a bargain security because he thinks the general market is going down still further is quite another question; and I think that is largely a personal matter. Our opinion is that for the investor it is better to have his money invested than it is to feel around for the bottom of the securities market. And if you can invest your money under fair conditions, in fact under attractive specific conditions, I think one certainly should do so even if the market should go down further and even if the securities you buy may also go down after you buy them. That is rather a long answer to this question, but it is an interesting one.

I might add another introductory statement: By a coincidence last week I noticed a news item with regard to the Taylorcraft Corporation, which was a company of which we gave a brief and unfavorable analysis at our first meeting. That company, you know, sold some stock on terms which we regarded as rather outrageous last summer. I find now they are in financial difficulties, and that trustees have been appointed. That is a rather extreme example of the value of security analysis. (Laughter)

Our purpose tonight is to start our discussion of the factor of future earnings in the analysis of securities. In the past two lectures we spoke more or less exclusively about the analysis of the past earnings. Of course, volumes can be written on that question now before us. It is not our purpose to cover it in a comprehensive way, starting from scratch, but rather to assume that you are familiar with the general treatment of the future earnings component which we gave in "Security Analysis", and to subject it to a further scrutiny, particularly with respect to what may have happened in the last few years in that sector.

I would like to start with something that would appeal to at least two members of this class, and that is with a definition of the term "earning power." That term has been used so loosely that I am ready to start a movement for its official abolition in Wall Street. When somebody asserts that a stock has an earning power of so much, I am sure that the person who hears him doesn't know what he means, and there is a good chance that the man who uses it doesn't know what it means.

My suggestion is that we use two phrases: One is "past earning power," and the other is "future earning power." Past earning power is certainly definite enough and it should mean the average earnings over a stated period which would ordinarily be identified in the discussion. But if not so identified it would be some representative period such as five or seven or perhaps ten years in the past. That would be the meaning of "past earning power."

When you are talking about future earning power, you should mean the average expectable earnings over some period in the future. I think most of us ought to think pretty much alike as to the period that we would talk about. My suggestion is that it would be a five-year period, and that when we speak of future earning power of a company, we should have in mind ordinarily the average earnings over the next five years. I say "ordinarily" because you have situations in which a company may be subject to abnormal conditions affecting earning power for some years to come; and there it may be desirable to make a further distinction. We shall talk later about the analysis of a building company stock, in which you might very well make some distinction between the earning power for a boom period, which is ahead perhaps for several years to come, and the earning power for a normal period, if there is such a thing in the building company industry. But apart from some special type of situation such as that, (and a war period such as we have gone through,) I think the use of "future earning power" to mean earnings expected for the next five years would be useful as a general expression.

As far as the use of earning power or earning prospects in Wall Street is concerned, let me point out that in most of the current thinking earning power is not considered along the lines of an average over a period of time of medium duration. It is either considered as the earnings that are being realized just now, or those right around the corner, such as the next twelve months; or else the earnings are considered in terms of the long and almost endless future.

A company with good prospects, for example, is supposed to be a company which will go on and on, more or less indefinitely increasing its earnings; and therefore it is not necessary to be too precise about what earnings you are talking about when you are considering the company's future. Actually that idea of the long-term future of companies with good prospects shows itself, not in the use of any particular earnings, but in the use of the multiplier which is applied to the recent earnings or to the average earnings of the past.

I am reminded of an analysis that we used in this course in 1939, in the very first lecture, which I believe illustrates that pretty well. We put on the board three companies: A, B, and C. Two of them, which we did not name, showed earnings of practically identical amounts for the last five years --$3.50

a share in each case. The earnings year by year were closely
similar. The only difference was that one stock was selling at
14 and the other was selling at 140. The stock that was selling
at 140 was Dow Chemical; the one that was selling at 14 was
Distillers Seagrams.

Obviously, the difference between 14 and 140 meant that
the market believed that the prospects for Dow Chemical were very
good and those for Distillers Seagrams were indifferent or worse
than that. This judgment showed itself in the use of a multiplier
of four in one case and a multiplier of forty in the other.

I think that represents a very dangerous kind of
thinking in Wall Street, and one which the security analyst
should get as far away from as he can. For if you are going to
project Dow's earnings practically to the year 2000 and determine
values that way, then of course you can justify any price that
you wish to. In fact, what actually happens is that you take
the price first, which happens to be not only the present market
but some higher price if you are bullish on the stock, and then
you determine a multiplier which will justify that price. That
procedure is the exact opposite of what a good security analyst
should do.

I think if a person had tried to project the earnings
of Dow Chemical for a five-year period and the earnings of
Distillers Seagrams for a five-year period, and compared them, he
could not have gotten values which would have justified the price
differential as great as ten to one in the two companies. It is
always an advantage to give examples of this sort that have such a
brilliant sequel; because I notice that this year Distillers
Seagrams sold as high as 150 as compared with its earlier price
of 14, and Dow Chemical sold as high as about 190, against 140--
which is quite a difference in relative behavior.

We have been trying to point out that this concept of
an indefinitely favorable future is dangerous, even if it is true;
because even if it is true you can easily overvalue the security,
since you make it worth anything you want it to be worth. Beyond
this, it is particularly dangerous too, because sometimes your
ideas of the future turn out to be wrong. Then you have paid an
awful lot for a future that isn't there. Your position then is
pretty bad. There will be other examples of that sort which we
may take up as we go along.

Let me now get back a little more closely to the work
of the security analyst, and ask the question, "What is the
relationship of this concept of future earning power to the
day-to-day, careful work of the security analyst, and his attitude
toward security values?" That relationship has developed gradually
over a period of years, and at a somewhat more significant rate in
the last few years.

It is interesting to go back in one's thinking to the
elements from which we started our ideas of the value of securities,--say, a generation ago or more than that. When I came
down to the Street, the thing everybody started with in valuations
was par value. That did not mean, of course, that a stock was
worth its par value. It might be worth more or less. But it was
considered as being worth a percentage of its par value. So much
was this true -- I don't know how many of you are aware of this --
that prior to about 1916 stocks were regularly quoted on the stock
exchange, not in dollars per share, but in percentage of their par
value. Westinghouse and Pennsylvania would sell, say, at 150,
which meant they were selling at $75 a share--because their par
value was 50. I suppose we have gotten so far away from par
values now that the only people who are interested in them are
those who calculate transfer taxes on securities. Because of
that tax reason, one-cent par values are regarded as a very smart
procedure in Wall Street today.

I can imagine the attitude of the old-fashioned investor
were he to buy a stock for fifty dollars and looked at the
certificate and found its par value was one cent. He would probably have fallen in a faint. Well, through many stages in a
long period of development from that rather naive attitude toward
the central point of value, you have come now to what might seem
to be the ultimate stage where the central point of value is the
future earnings power,--something which you cannot read on any
certificate. In fact, you cannot read it anywhere.

There is often a question in my mind whether we have
really made so much progress in moving on from the physical to
the almost metaphysical in this way; but be that as it may, we
have. And now it is the law of the land that the values of
securities, if they must be determined for the purpose of judging
fairness of any kind of transaction, will be based primarily on
the capitalization of expected future earnings. That is the
burden of the famous Consolidated Rock Products case that you
see referred to all the time in SEC proceedings, and in other
cases of similar character.

When the Supreme Court says it is a fact that the value
depends upon future earning power, that does not mean that the
test of the value that the Supreme Court has laid down as the law
on this subject has therefore become the proper test for us security analysts. I think rather that we have laid down the law to
the Supreme Court. That is to say, the Supreme Court has said
that the values are now to be determined primarily in relation to
future earning power, because it has observed that values have
actually been determined by buyers and sellers of securities more
and more in relation to such expected earnings.

The Supreme Court had lagged behind the times for quite
a while in that matter, and it just caught up. I think perhaps
that it is still lagging behind the times in some other respects.

The concept that investment value is dependent upon expected future earnings is undoubtedly a more persuasive and a more logical one than thinking of value in relation to past earnings only, or in relation to the par value printed on the certificate, or any other stage in between. But I must emphasize to you that this concept does not make the job of the security analyst easier. On the contrary, it makes it a great deal harder, and it places him in a serious dilemma, for now the past earnings, with which he can become very closely familiar and which he can study with a great deal of skill and ingenuity, --those past earnings unfortunately are not determinative of value. And the element which is determinative of value, the future earnings, is just the thing which he cannot analyze with any real feeling of assurance as to the correctness of his conclusions.

That would be a very sad dilemma indeed for us security analysts if it were not for that principle of continuity that I tried to emphasize in the first lecture. While it is true that it is the expected future earnings and not the past that determines value, it is also true that there tends to be a rough relationship or continuing connection between past earnings and future earnings. In the typical case, therefore, it is worthwhile for the analyst to pay a great deal of attention to the past earnings, as the beginning of his work, and to go on from those past earnings to such adjustments for the future as are indicated by his further study.

You all know, of course, that the dependability of past earnings as a guide to the future is sufficient to make it possible to rely almost exclusively on them in the selection of a high-grade investment bond or preferred stock. We have said, in fact, that you cannot properly buy such an investment security on the basis of expected earnings, where these are very different from past earnings--and where you are relying on new developments, as it were, to make the security sound, when it would not have been sound on the basis of the past.

But you may say, conversely, that if you buy it on the basis of the past and the new developments turn out to be disappointing, you are running the risk of having made an unwise investment. We find from experience, though, that where the past margin of safety that you demand for your security is high enough, in practically every such case the future will measure up sufficiently close to the past to make your investment a sound one. This type of investment will not require any great gifts of prophesy, any great shrewdness with regard to anticipating the future. In fact, it would be a very unfortunate thing if you could not get two and three-quarters per cent on your money without having to be something of a soothsayer as far as the future earnings of corporations is concerned.

When I make that statement, of course I do not mean to lay down the inflexible rule that any company that gives you a sufficiently great margin in its past earnings can be regarded as having sound securities for investment. If the investor has occasion to be fearful of the future of such a company, it is perfectly logical for him to obey his fears and pass on from that enterprise to some other security about which he is not so fearful. But the point I am making -- and I hope you can understand it, -- is that in the selection of high-grade securities you start with a demand for an adequate coverage in past earnings; and in the typical case that is sufficient to justify the selection of the bond.

I think I might pause there to see whether any questions have arisen in your mind on that point, before I go on from that rather simple application to its more complicated application to the valuation of common stocks.

In the case of common stocks the technique of security analysis has made rather important progress from the rather hit-and-miss method of taking past earnings as a guide and then saying, "Well, I think the future is pretty good here, so I'll multiply the earnings by a higher than average multiplier." Or in the converse case: "I think the future is not so good, so I'll multiply these past earnings by a lower amount."

It is now becoming approved practice in any really good analysis to work out the future earning power along somewhat independent lines, --by considering afresh the most important factors on which the earning power will depend. These factors in the ordinary case are not very numerous. They consist, first, of the physical output or volume of business that you expect from the company. Secondly, the price, or unit price, that it will get. Thirdly, its unit cost; and then, fourth, the tax rate. We now have a standard technique by which you go through these various motions and set up these successive figures, --all of which are estimates, of course. By this operation you arrive at a conclusion as to future earning power. That is regarded, and should be regarded, as a better technique than the simple one of merely taking the past earnings over a period of time.

Consequently, when you undertake a full-scale analysis of a security and want to determine whether it should be bought or not -- I should say, frankly, whether it should be bought or sold -- your proper technique should consist of estimating the future earning power along the lines that I have mentioned, and then applying a multiplier to it which is influenced in part by your subjective ideas as to the security, but which has to be kept within a reasonable range of variation.

It is not, I assure you, admissible security-analysis technique to say, "I don't like this company, so I will multiply the future earnings by four; but I do like the other company so I will multiply the future earnings by forty." You will not get a passing grade on a security-analysis test if you do anything of that kind. But naturally there is room for some variation in your multiplier as applied to these earnings. When you use that multiplier, you arrive at a valuation which can be a guide to you in your attitude toward the stock.

I was going to go on with some other examples of that method, but I find that I have left out a little note that I put on one of my pages headed "The Digression." This was intended to contribute somewhat to your amusement and edification.

You may recall that I have been emphasizing the difficulty of peering into the future and coming through with some good ideas as to what will happen. Let me now indicate to you the position of somebody who really could have looked in the crystal ball and derived a good deal of dependable information about the future. Let us see how well he would have fared. I am assuming that each of you was one of these fortunate investors who really had a crystal ball, and could foretell in 1939 that different groups of stocks would expand their business in the percentages that we show on the blackboard here.

Now, we say, suppose you were also told that in September 1946 the general level of industrial prices (as shown by the SEC calculations) would be 29 per cent higher than they were in January 1939. That happens to be true. Consequently the stocks in these groups would vary around a center of a 29 per cent advance. Suppose, then, you were asked back in 1939, "What would be the change in the prices of these securities by 1946?" Here, for example, is Aircraft Manufacturing, which is expanding thirty-one times in volume, from 1939 to 1944. Here is Aviation Transport which is expanding two and a half times. I could, for our amusement, ask you to make what you would regard as a reasonable estimate of the change in market prices from January 1939 to September 1946; but instead of going through that rigmarole I shall merely give you the results.

At September 16, 1946, the Aviation Transport securities were up 274 per cent from January 1939--which was pretty good, I should say, compared with 240 per cent increase in business. But the aircraft manufacturing companies were down 74 per cent. I do not think you would have expected that if you had known the relative change in sales. Amusement stocks and Tobacco products both benefitted just about the same in gross from the war conditions. But the difference was that the Amusement stocks advanced 242 percent and the Tobacco stocks declined 10-1/2 per cent,-- which is quite a difference.

The Tire and Rubber companies did not do as well as Electric Manufacturing in sales, but in price they went up 85 per cent while the electric machinery equipment went up only 2 per cent.

Metal and Metal Mining did not do quite as well as Paper in sales expansion. But the difference here is also rather surprising, because the Paper and Allied Products stocks increased 107 per cent in value, and the Metal Mining stocks declined 6 per cent during that period.

CHANGES IN SALES VOLUME COMPARED WITH CHANGES IN STOCK
PRICES FOR VARIOUS INDUSTRIAL GROUPS.

GROUP	Sales Increase 1944 vs 1939	Change in Group Stock Price Index Sept. 16, 1946 vs Jan. 1939
Aircraft Mfg.	+ 3070%	- 7.4%
Air Transport	+ 240	+ 273.8
Amusement	+ 72	+ 247.8
Tobacco Mfg.	+ 75	- 10.5
Elec. Mach. & Equip.	+ 318	+ 2.0
Tire & Rubber	+ 220	+ 85.3
Metals and Mining	+ 60	- 5.9
Paper & Allied	+ 100	+ 107.8
All Stocks		+ 28.6

You see that the discrepancies in market movement are so great that they should add an extra note of caution in our attitudes toward our future calculations. For even if we knew what was going to happen to a company, in terms of its business and its earning power, we might not be able to make too good a prediction as to what was going to happen to it in the market price, which interests us a good deal. That is just an added reason for being either as cautious as possible in regard to our own decisions on security purchases, or else protecting ourselves as much as we can in our own thinking and in our statements by qualifying comments, whenever we begin to make predictions as to the future.

Now I should like to go on and give you a detailed example of the kind of analysis which is now being made, that centers around an estimate of futre earnings and works on from there to a valuation. I have two examples here. One of them relates to the Childs Company. That happens to be rather convenient because here we have our good friend, the Securities and Exchange Commission, sweating through a valuation of the Childs Company which is based primarily upon their estimate of future earnings. They do this because they have to. They are required to find out the comparative values of the preferred and common stocks in their report to the court on the fairness of the proposed

reorganization plans. The only way they know of of determining
the comparative value is by getting the total value of the enterprise and then comparing that with the claim of the preferred
stock. And so they go through an elaborate technique in order to
value the Childs Preferred and Common shares.

It might be worthwhile now to take a little time and see
just how they have done it. Perhaps I should make the matter a
little clearer to you. The Childs Company, most of you know, has
been in trusteeship. The company is now evidently solvent, and
can easily take care of its debts. So the problem of reorganization
actually turns upon giving the proper amounts of new securities
to the old preferred and common stock.

The SEC, in its wisdom, decided that the capitalization
of the preferred and common stock should be changed from what it
was before. It is thus necessary to determine what proportion of
a new common-stock issue, if that is to be the only stock, should
go to the preferred and what to the common. The problem before
the SEC, then, was to determine what the whole enterprise was
worth. If the preferred stock claim was 75 per cent of such
value, for example, they would then allot 75 per cent of the stock
to the preferred and the balance to the common.

What they did was to start with a projection of the
sales of Childs, which they took at $18,000,000, somewhat less
than the figures for 1945,--they assuming that business would
not be as good in the long-term future as it was under war conditions. They then took a percentage of profit of 6 per cent before
taxes. That was based upon a study of profit margins both for this
company and for other restaurant companies; and I do not believe
that analysts would be likely to differ very much with them. So
they got a net before taxes of $1,100,000.

Then they subtracted the expected average tax rates.
Here the SEC decided to cut down the current rate of 38 per cent
to 35,--a very valiant gesture of guessing. The main question,
in estimating the tax rate, was whether it was likely that the
great pressure to eliminate double taxation on corporations would
be effective in the future in such a way, perhaps, as to relieve
corporations of either all or most of the tax. Their guess, and
mine too, was that such was not likely to happen, desirable as it
might be.

So the net after tax was estimated at $715,000. That
is the future earning power, and you can see that is a relatively
simple calculation. It represents smaller earnings than Childs
had during the war period before taxes, but considerably more than
in the pre-war period.

I might pause here and ask whether there are any questions that come up on this rather simple demonstration of the
determination of expected future earnings.

QUESTION: How do they estimate the future sales?

MR. GRAHAM: Well, here is sort of a summary of a rather long discussion about the effect of retaining some restaurants, closing others and opening up others. They say, "Considering the record of the fifty-three units" -- which includes some which would be closed -- "and giving weight to the various factors that affect future sales to the chain, we believe that the management forecast of $20,000,000 restaurant sales for the average future year is excessive. For such a figure to be achieved, the chain would have to average in good years and bad years sales which would be ten per cent higher than those achieved by the fifty-three restaurants in 1945, which in turn were higher than in any previous recent year for more than a decade. It is true that in 1946, with the first six months' results known, the management estimated that the sales will exceed $21,400,000. However, it must be recognized that the company is experiencing extraordinarily high retail sales and Childs' current high sales level cannot be considered to correspond to the level which may reasonably be forecast for a normal year in the future." "We believe however, even giving consideration to normal retail business, that the chain can reasonably be anticipated to average sales of $18,000,000, which was the amount realized in 1945 by the fifty-three restaurants --" The conclusion is a rather interesting point of technique. Rather than take a figure completely out of the air, you go back to the earnings of a past year which you think will correspond to a typical future year and arrive at the figures that way.

QUESTION: Wouldn't the common stock holders have a basis of argument about the sales and therefore throw out the whole business?

MR. GRAHAM: You mean can they argue against that?

QUESTION: Yes. Well, they can say it is higher; it should be 21 million, or whatever it was in 1946.

MR. GRAHAM: Well, your point is perfectly right. The common stock holders can say that, and so could the SEC have said it -- but they didn't. And when you get down to the judicial question on which this matter turns, here is what the courts say on a matter of that kind: They would say that the SEC is competent and impartial; that their guess is probably a better guess than one advanced by an interested party such as a common-stock holder. But if the common stock people could adduce very convincing evidence,--not merely an insistent argument--which would show that the estimate is out of line with normal expectancy, then the SEC's figures could be rejected by the court.

QUESTION: Did the trustee represent the common stock-holder's viewpoint here?

MR. GRAHAM: No, a trustee wouldn't normally represent just the common stock. The SEC assumed Child's Trustee's views were too liberal. In other cases, the Commission has considered the Trustee's estimate as not liberal enough.

QUESTION: Didn't the SEC introduce the price level in their computations somewhere?

MR. GRAHAM: Not in any explicit calculation.

QUESTION: By using the 1945 level they might discount what they consider to be a bulge in food prices right now.

MR. GRAHAM: Perhaps they do refer to the fact, in their analysis of merchandise costs, that there has been a scarcity of supplies, and that the opportunities to purchase food and liquor at bargain prices have disappeared during war years.

QUESTION: Let me ask another question, then: From your observation isn't retail merchandising, whether it is a restaurant chain or anything else, strictly a matter of percentages? In other words, give them a price level, they work both their costs and selling prices up and down accordingly.

MR. GRAHAM: It generally works out that way. This six percent figure which they give for net before taxes is based pretty much upon average experience in the past. I presume that is the percentage you are referring to. We know, for example, that food in the typical restaurant represents anywhere between one-third and 40 per cent of the total sales check. Once a stable price level has been established, that percentage tends to be established again, even if it was set aside for a while because of sudden changes in price level. For Child's merchandise costs have risen from 34.7% in 1938 to 38.5% in 1945.

QUESTION: No question that the prevailing prices that this chain has to deal with in '46 would be higher than in '45? No question in your mind, is there?

MR. GRAHAM: No.

QUESTION: And that automatically would govern in actual volume of sales, wouldn't it?

MR. GRAHAM: It would unless for some reason the customers were driven away from restaurants, which so far I don't think the figures show. But '46, of course, is not regarded necessarily as a typical postwar year by the SEC, and probably correctly so.

These questions are really good questions, not so much as criticisms of what the SEC does, as they are indications of the necessary degree of uncertainty involved in any such procedure. The only thing you can say in favor of it is that something of this kind must be done. The SEC must do it as intelligently as they can; and you as security analysts must also do it intelligently. But don't ever think that because you go through some very careful operations and work things out to two or three decimal places, as I sometimes see it done, that you have got an accurate and precise idea as to what will happen in the future. You just don't have any such thing. It isn't there.

There were some other hands raised on this question of Childs.

QUESTION: I would like to raise the question of working with post-tax margins rather than pre-tax margins to avoid the dilemma of estimating what the tax rate will be, on the theory that competition will drive the post-tax margin down to about what it was.

MR. GRAHAM: There has been a great deal of discussion in academic circles on the incidence of the corporation tax,-- as to whether it is really paid by the consumer or whether it is paid by the prosperous corporation as compared with a non-profitable corporation that couldn't have to pay any tax. That matter is still very controversial, and apparently the SEC prefers to follow the assumption that the margin should be calculated before tax. In practice, it didn't make much difference, since they used practically the current tax.

Were there any other questions about that?

We are really going on further in the Childs' matter, than the mere matter of estimating future earnings; because I think we ought to follow it through to its conclusion by the SEC, and perhaps by ourselves as sitting in judgment on the SEC.

They next came to the multiplier and they said that their multiplier should be twelve and a half. That is to say, a capitalization rate of eight per cent, which gave them a value of about nine million dollars for the company on an earnings basis. I don't think much was said that would illuminate the question of why they selected a multiplier of twelve and a half. They reject the Trustees' multiplier of ten. That is the first thing they do. Then they add one of those precious clauses that you find in the Tax Court almost always, and in the SEC frequently. They say, "Giving consideration to all the factors, including rates of capitalization which have prevailed for other restaurant chains, it is our conclusion that estimated net earnings of $1,100,000 before income taxes and $715,000 after income taxes can fairly be capitalized at rates approximately twelve per cent and eight per cent respectively, resulting in a capitalized earnings figure of about $9,000,000."

That means that using their best judgment they will multiply the earnings after taxes by twelve and a half. I assure

you that the alternative capitalization of earnings before taxes
was figured out at a rate to correspond with their capitalization
of the earnings after taxes. I think it was put in there, because
in the McKesson and Robbins case they were led by the Trustees'
calculations there to do some valuation of earnings before taxes--
something that had never been done before, as far as I know.
Their capitalization rate, of course, is pretty much an arbitrary
matter, and yet I assume that most analysts would not get very
far away from their multiplier.

QUESTION: They use a lower times multiplier than the
trustees. Is that the effect of that?

MR. GRAHAM: No, a higher multiplier. They cut down his
earnings somewhat, and they increase his multiplier so I think
they end up pretty near the same evaluation.

QUESTION: You said eight times, didn't you?

MR. GRAHAM: No, an eight per cent figure. That eight
per cent is twelve and a half times. The trustee had used a
multiplier of ten.

QUESTION: And they were giving arguments against the
use of the ten per cent by the trustee?

MR. GRAHAM: Yes, but the matter is too complicated to
take up here. The Trustee had used what he called a "segmental
method", in which he considered that part of it was equivalent to
bonds, another part to preferred stock, another part to common
stock, and the SEC argues about it. Incidentally, you should
know that the SEC goes at these things very seriously. I mean,
their valuation isn't so much of a rule of thumb way as you may
think from my description,--though I have a little mental reser-
vation on that, and believe that you might get pretty much the
same results by rule of thumb method. But they certainly don't
do it that way. When they start with analysis of estimates of
earnings, they have a discussion of about three pages on the
management factor. Then they have three pages on the sales, half
a page on merchandise costs, half a page on labor costs, then
paragraphs on other costs, on building operating profits, on
depreciation and rentals, on overhead. Then, after all those
discussions, they reach this calculation of six per cent of the
sales of $18,000,000. Evidently, a great deal of work of the
staff went into this.

Thus they got a valuation of nine million dollars,
based upon earning power. Then they went through some motions
after that, on some of which I part company very definitely with
the SEC. First they figure out some tax savings due to carry-
backs and things of that sort, and they say they will get
$1,200,000 from that. Then they say they have to spend $1,800,000
for rehabilitation of the restaurants, so they subtract that. And

therefore they reduce their $9,000,000 by $600,000 net and get
$8,400,000. That is their net value by the earnings method.

Then they add excess working capital and unneeded real
estate to that figure. From their calculations these amount to
$5,100,000, and so they get a final total value of $13,500,000.
They have to deduct from this $13,500,000, the funded debt of
$3,200,000. So they get a net value for stock of $10,300,000.
They value the preferred stocks' claim at par and back dividends,
amounting to $7,649,000. Thus the balance left for common would
be $2,656,000.

Consequently they reach the conclusion that, if one
class of stock is to be issued, then somewhere between seventy
and seventy-five per cent of the total should be given to the
preferred stock and somewhere between twenty-five and thirty
per cent should be given to the common. That happens to be an
unusually modest type of conclusion for the SEC. In the past they
have generally come out with an elaborate calculation and said:
"We believe that 72.45% of this company should go to the preferred
and the balance of 27.55% to the common." But I think they are
getting a little mellow and are realizing that their calculations
are pretty much estimates and should be turned into round amounts.

As a practical matter it turned out that the reorganization is now being carried through on close to the SEC's basis,
although the original plans which were proposed by the Trustee
and by a number of other people for the most part departed very
substantially from these proportions. I won't teke the time to
tell you what the different plans were; but the Trustee now
allocates 76-2/3% of the new stock to the preferred.

Let us stop here and proceed a little further with
the Childs' case at our next meeting.

Lecture No. 5   December 3, 1946.

CURRENT PROBLEMS IN SECURITY ANALYSIS

By
Benjamin Graham
****

As a preliminary perhaps I might answer any questions
that are in your mind growing out of the last lecture, which ended
rather precipitously. Does anyone have anything on his mind? We
were discussing the Childs' valuation by the Securities and Exchange
Commission. At that time, you will recall, we had indicated that
the SEC had valued the Childs Company primarily on the basis of
its future earning power, which was the thing that interested us,
but had added a certain amount for excess working capital--
actually $1,300,000 net after paying the bonds. Let me make the
point here that a security analyst would not be inclined to add in
the excess working capital to the valuation of the property unless
he believed that the money was to be returned in some way or other
to security holders. As a matter of fact, some part of the excess
working capital was to be used to pay off the old debt of Childs,
and that portion, of course, represented an addition to the earning-
power value of the old company. Thus our own "practical" valuation
would tend to be $9,000,000 rather than the $10,000,000 found by
the S.E.C.

Since we discussed the matter two weeks ago, the Federal
Court has approved the Childs' plan, based upon the modified
proposals of the trustee; and it has apparently placed the stock
equity at $9,980,000, which is $300,000 less than the amount that
the SEC found.

It may be interesting to look a bit at the prices of the
securities, to see what they indicate as of now. The preferred and
common together were selling for about $8,400,000 yesterday,
preferred at 155 and the common at 7-1/8. This is less than the
valuations that we have been talking about. There is nothing
surprising about that, of course; because it is a normal experience
to have the securities of a company in trusteeship sell at less
than the valuations that an analyst would find for the property
on a reorganized basis. It would be expected that the value would
normally increase over a period of time -- such as one year or
two years, following trusteeship, -- as the enterprise gains its
proper position in the public's esteem. That is almost an
invariable experience.

Another way of looking at it might be to say that while
the multiplier of the earnings of $715,000 might well be twelve and

a half on a settled or seasoned basis, at the present time the multiplier might be as little as ten,--in which case the value would be only seven million and a quarter.

There is one other factor in these prices which some of you may have noticed, namely that the preferred stock price is out of line with the common. The relative new securities given represent about 28-1/2 to 1 in favor of the preferred stock. Hence if the preferred stock is worth only 155, the common would be worth only about 5-1/2,-- as against a current price of somewhat over seven.

QUESTION: When was that base established, that twelve and a half times earnings, on what date?

MR. GRAHAM: That report of the SEC is dated September 30, 1946, which is fairly recent.

The fact that the common stock is selling higher in relation to the preferred than the terms of the exchange would warrant also is not at all extraordinary. In fact, that is almost standard experience down in Wall Street. In these reorganization matters common stock which gets small recognition generally tends to sell in the market for more than it is offered in the plan. This happens partly because people who deal in low-priced common stocks are not generally very careful analysts and do not pay a great deal of attention to the arithmetic of a complicated plan; partly, also, because efforts are often made to improve the position of the common stock, and speculators are willing to take some chance on the success of such efforts.

There have been some cases during the rising markets of the last few years in which these efforts have been successful. And so the speculators were justified in paying more for the common than the plan offered it. However, I doubt whether a great deal of careful calculation of this sort goes into the Childs case, because we are not now in the type of market in which one is likely to get better treatment than a court has given to common stock. I know from experience that in many other cases the common stocks have sold too high almost at the very moment when their value was to be determined once for all, by the actual physical exchange.

One interesting case is Pittsburgh Coal, in which you had a situation very much like this in 1945. At the very moment when the exchange was to be made and the old common stock was to be stricken from the list, there was a similar discrepancy in market price.

That question, of course, is not closely related to our primary interest at this time, which is the matter of valuation of a company based upon estimates of future earning power. But I think, as I said two weeks ago, it is a good idea for us to try to carry through our discussions of corporations and to reach a fairly rounded conclusion with respect to them.

Are there any questions about this matter, primarily this question of the valuation of Childs, based upon the capitalization of its expected future earnings?

QUESTION: That twelve and a half times seems awfully high. I can't see how they ever got a twelve and a half times base for a company that had such a horrible record.

MR. GRAHAM: Well, the record of Childs is not really horrible, especially not in their most recent years. They make a statement that the management of Childs has not been as good as it should have been and, therefore, there is an opportunity for ample improvement over the past. If you compare Childs with Bickford and Waldorf, you will observe that all three companies have about the same amount of sales last year, Childs having somewhat more. The earnings of Childs have been better in relation to sales than the other two companies, and the values of the stocks of Waldorf and Bickford would justify a $9,000,000 valuation for Childs, as the following figures would show: Childs earned $1,368,000 in 1945; Waldorf, $795,000; Bickford, $1,015,000. Waldorf is selling for about eight million; Bickford about eight million two, including debt. So that I think the nine-million-dollar valuation would be justified there.

I think you would be right in assuming that the stock would not sell at twelve and a half times earnings immediately, especially where the aura of bankruptcy still surrounds it; but I do not think the SEC was wrong in assuming that it could sell at that price in the future. That is what they generally base their valuations on: not the immediate value but the ultimate settled value.

Any other questions about that?

Now let us go on again to this question of valuation of companies based on future earnings, by taking another concern not in trusteeship. It is one which, by coincidence, I happen to have seen a good many circulars on, which came to my desk in the last year, and that is the American Radiator -- Standard Sanitary Corporation. Looking through my files, I discovered no less than five discussions of this company, and they are interesting as throwing some light upon the way in which Wall Street goes at its analyses of corporation, and some light perhaps on the way it should or should not go at them.

The first one that I have -- and there is no particular point in identifying by name, so we shall just call it number one-- is dated December 12, 1945 and is headed "The Building Situation." It gives a great deal of information about building securities and includes a number of references to a number of building stocks, such as American Raditor Standard Sanitary. It implies that these companies should be bought, the price of Radiator then being 18-1/4. Now, this is a rather peculiar kind of analysis, because it is filled with a great deal of material on the industry but it does not relate this material in any way to the prices of the stocks which it lists. Hence everything that is said might be perfectly true, and it probably was; yet I do not see how anyone could tell from it whether American Radiator, as an example, would be attractive or unattractive at 19. If the implication was that it was attractive simply because the building industry was sound, then it might be attractive at 190 instead of at 19. That is one type of analysis, which does not include any calculation of the future earning power of the company, but does give you an elaborate projection of the possibilities of the industry as a whole.

The next one, number two, is rather interesting, because it not only gives the conventional statement of the company's exhibit for a ten-year period and the conventional description of the company's business and reference to various possibilities that might affect it, but it also has the ingenious or ingenuous idea of listing favorable and unfavorable factors, one against the other. There are seven favorable and four unfavorable.

Now I think the only way in which you could tell what their real opinion was of this stock would be by assuming it from the fact that there were seven favorable factors and only four unfavorable factors. Outside of that partiality it is a master-piece of description without reaching any conclusion. I would say that it undoubtedly serves a useful purpose. What they are saying, virtually in terms, is: "We are not going to express an opinion about this company, but you can form your own opinion based upon what we tell you."

The third, which I have here, is dated April 12, 1946. It gives a rather sketchy account of the building industry; it gives the usual ten-year figures for the American Radiator Company; and ends with the following conclusion: "American Raditor, one of the largest building-industry companies, with extensive facilities, will have the opportunity to take full advantage of the anticiated heavy demand for building products and should, on this basis, show increased earnings. On the basis of the foregoing, the common stock appears attractive as a speculation at current levels."

The criticism of that conclusion is two-fold. In the first place, the statement made that the company is likely to show increased earnings because of the anticipated heavy demand for building products is a completely obvious one. Everybody, even people in Wall Street, must have known that the building industry was facing a heavy demand; and to say simply that because it faces a heavy demand it is an attractive speculation would seem pretty much on the naive side. It would assume that the brokerage firms were the only people who knew that this company was going into a period of this sort.

Another criticism is this: If the figures for a ten-year period are supplied in such detail, it might be assumed that they were supplied for the purpose of relating the figures to the price, to what you are getting for your money. Since no reference is made to any such relationship, we might infer that the figures are only put there for window dressing, and the main object was to say the stock looks pretty good as a speculation in today's market. If so, the circular might as well have been limited to that.

The fourth analysis that I have really comes in two parts: One is an analysis dated February 6, 1946, which was put out by a research corporation; and then it appears again in another circular dated October 23, 1946, put out by a stock exchange firm. This represents a really good effort at research and evaluation. My purpose in giving you all these circulars is to indicate at what different levels analysis is being carried on in Wall Street, pretty much at the same time.

Here we have a five-page discussion of American Radiator, in which a great deal of information is supplied on the industry,--not only its past, but future calculations, based upon somebody else's estimates for the year 1947; and also some other estimates for the years running between 1946 and '51, on the demand and supply of new houses.

Then they take up the earning power of American Radiator Company; and for the first time in this group of analyses that we are speaking of they actually endeavor to determine what the value of the company would be, based on assumptions as to earning power and as to multipliers. Their method is as follows: They project sales at the rate of $160,000,000; and this, you see, is our now familiar Childs Company method. Then they apply a profit margin, which they expect to be fifteen per cent. Then they say, "Net per stock: $1.40 per share." They do not give you the arithmetic of that, but here it is: Net before taxes would be $24,000,000, less taxes at about forty per cent, brings it down to about fourteen million-odd, and that is about a dollar forty on ten million shares of stock. Then they add: "Foreign earnings, estimated twenty-five cents" -- and that is a very rough estimate. So they get a dollar sixty to a dollar seventy per share, total. Further, they state that the earnings of a dollar sixty-five should begin to appear within the relatively near future,--and because these favorable earnings should continue over a considerable period of time, the stock of this company should prove to be relatively attractive even at its present level, the "present level" being about 20, in February, 1946.

That analysis was later used by a stock exchange house, which concludes, without needing quite as much courage, that the stock looks relatively attractive at 15, which was the price on October 23, 1946.

Now, before I attempt a criticism, not necessarily unfavorable, of this analysis, I may as well go on to the last one that reached my desk, which is headed "Active Years Ahead for the Building Industry." It gives a great deal of information on the building industry, and information about the companies in the industry, including American Radiator, which is the first one. There they make a calculation of the earning power of the company in what they call year 194x, which they figure at $1.75 per share. They use an expected profit margin of twelve per cent. There is a little discrepency between the 12% and their final result. It can be explained, if you want to go to the trouble, partly because they take into account foreign earnings to a greater extent than did the research company analysis.

Now, the interesting thing about this analysis is two-fold: First they get earnings of about a dollar seventy-five, which is not so different from the other projection. But they describe that estimate as follows: "A rough guess of potential earning power under optimum conditions over the next few years is shown by the line designated 194x." In the rest of the circular, while not too specific, they imply that these stocks are attractive, the ones that they have listed, because of the expected earnings in the 194x year. That is particularly true because the price of American Radiator was only thirteen and a half on that date, and the estimated earnings of a dollar seventy-five would make the price of thirteen and a half look quite reasonable if that represented future earning power.

My comment on these analyses -- the last two ones, which are the only ones that seriously attempt a projection of future earnings -- is this: They do not emphasize enough the fact that the earnings they are dealing with are earnings of a boom period; but the technique of analysis should take that carefully into account.

The earnings for the building boom should be evaluated pretty much in the same way as we were accustomed to evaluating war earnings, that is to say, by assuming that they were to last for a limited number of years. The excess earnings during that period should be added to what we would assume to be the normal valuation of the company based upon its average peacetime earnings. Thus, if you want to attempt a serious evaluation of a company like American Radiator, the only proper method is to take what you would assume to be its normal earning power, not its optimum earning power, evaluate that, and then add to it a fair allowance for the fact that it is facing some very good years.

I might say that if you want to be somewhat pessimistic you could criticize even that method; because you might argue that these boom years are simply part of a building cycle period, -- they are not really excess earnings; they are the good part of the normal earnings and will be offset by very low earnings when the building boom subsidies. That comment may be justified; but in any event the method that I spoke of before seems to me to be as liberal a method as you could use.

You had a question about that?

QUESTION: What makes you say that in that estimate of 160 million dollars of sales, those factors were not considered?

MR. GRAHAM: You mean the fact that they were boom period sales?

QUESTION: Possibly they did consider that.

MR. GRAHAM: I can give you a specific reason for that. They say that the earnings are related closely to the residential building totals that will be expected. And over the period 1946-51 they have gone to the trouble of giving you a projection of the amount of buildings needed and the amount that will be supplied. During the years '47-51 they are expecting a million units of building annually. At the end of that time the deficiency will be completely remedied; and, on the basis of their statistics, demand would be reduced to where around 550,000 buildings a year, that is to say, about half a million new families plus demolition. Following through this calculation to the year 1952, you would find that the expectation of new units would be not more than half of the one on which they had based their 160 million of dollars sales.

Another reason, of course, is that the sales actually realized in 1939 were only 80 million dollars, and in 1938 68 million. Thus the volume of 160 million, even allowing for some increase in prices, would obviously be on the high side.

Were there other questions about that? Questions of this kind are very good, because they help clarify the reasoning behind these evaluations.

It seems to me that the method of evaluation, then, should be somewhat different for American Radiator than has been used. You ought to start, not with the optimum earnings, but what you would consider to be normal earnings for the company.

The company had been earning on the order of about fifty cents a share in the period before the war; and I would assume that if you take earnings of a dollar a share after the war, you would be about as optimistic as you would have any right to be about this company's earnings after the building boom has subsided. I am inclined to think that is over-optimistic, as far as one can see now, for the very reason that when the building boom has subsided you are likely to go into a period of subnormal earnings if the building cycle behaves in the future as it has in the past. But if you accept the one-dollar earnings -- and I really want to mark that as liberal,-- I think the multiplier would be somewhere

between twelve and fifteen. That is higher than the company's past
record would justify,--but the American Radiator has some advantages in being a large and strong company, well thought of, and
which many years ago was a very large earner. Consequently, I
think you would get a valuation of $12 to $15 on a normal basis.

To that you would add an allowance for the boomtime
earnings, which are seventy-five cents a share over expected
normal. If you multiply this by four you are again pretty liberal;
that will give you three dollars extra. The valuation, thus
comes to about fifteen to eighteen dollars a share for the stock,
giving the company the benefit of certain doubts that I would
have in my own mind. This valuation, I think, could properly
have been made for American Radiator at any time during the past
year , and would have justified caution with regard to a purchase
of that stock for investment at the prices of early 1946.

But on that subject let me add that it is perfectly
proper to buy stocks for speculation. There is no crime in that.
When you buy stocks for speculation it is perfectly proper to
take speculative factors into account, which are different from
investment factors. The normal expectancy would be that if this
company is to earn a dollar seventy-five a share for three or four
years, the market will reflect those earnings in full on a speculative basis, without making allowance for the fact that they
are temporary.

That hasn't always happened. For example, during the
war the market certainly didn't reflect war earnings on the theory
that they were permanent earnings. But the market does tend to do
so with regard to cyclical earnings; it regards the boomtime
earnings as permanent earnings. For that reason it is quite
possible that American Radiator could sell, under good general
market conditions and during its own boom period, at a price
very much above our value of 15 to 18.

We must not forget that American Radiator as recently
as 1942 sold at 3-3/4. What we are saying is that American
Radiator is a speculative type of security by the nature of its
business, as well as by the fact that it is a common stock. Just
as it can sell at four dollars in a bad year, it can easily sell
at thirty dollars in a good year, and both prices would be
fundamentally justified. Our own valuation represents the type
of investment approach which tends pretty much to bring you what
you would consider to be a central value for the stock. This
interests the investor primarily; but second it may interest the
intelligent speculator too. For he could then see how far he is
getting away from central value when he is following up the
speculative aspects of the situation.

I welcome questions about that, because I think that is
very important.

QUESTION: If we are to estimate future earnings for just a period of five years, when you speak of a normal period for this industry, wouldn't your analysis go beyond that five-year period? The boom years might be the next five years. Then if you are striking for a normal level, that would go beyond the next five years; so as a result your earnings in the coming five years would be on a higher level and your normal period lower.

MR. GRAHAM: Yes, you are right in making that point. If my recollection is correct, I did make that point too, in my third lecture. I said that normally the earnings that you are trying to estimate are those of the next five years,--perhaps five to seven years,--but that there might be some exceptional cases. And I did have the building industry in mind, in which the next five years would not be regarded as a normal expectancy. The analyst is under a special disadvantage, then, because the normal earnings that you are thinking of lie so much further ahead in the future that your chance of being wrong in calculating what they are going to be is that much greater. But there is no help for it. You cannot properly evaluate the boom earnings of the next few years as normal; so you must jump ahead to the later earnings.

QUESTION: But when the market regards the earnings of a company, if the company went along for five years at a high rate of earnings, then wouldn't the market place a higher valuation on those earnings, considering the length of time the earnings would be at that high level?

MR. GRAHAM: Yes; because the market would tend to multiply the earnings by your standard multiplier of fifteen or thereabouts, instead of merely adding them in the way we suggest you do. (I am speaking, now, of the abnormal or excess component of those earnings.) The investor would then be out of step with the market in his attitude toward a stock like American Radiator.

The investor is very often out of step with the market, incidentally, and that would be no new experience for him. But I think it is useful for the investor to have some idea of what would seem to be the reasonable value, even if the current market may not reflect it at all.

QUESTION: Why do you use the multiplier four? I didn't hear why.

MR. GRAHAM: Oh, that was on the theory that there would be four boom years in the building industry. It is really based upon this calculation, which I think was rather carefully made: That the housing deficiency would be about over at the end of 1950, and that excess earnings would begin to be made around 1947.

QUESTION: What kind of an allowance would you make for the statement of an executive of this company at this particular

time? He did say the line that he is in could go along almost at
full production for two years just on replacements, modernization
and replacement. That wouldn't always be a factor, though, would
it, to that extent?

     MR. GRAHAM: No, I think the modernization would pro-
bably peter out along with the new construction. I believe they
go hand in hand.

     QUESTION: He called it replacement, but I guess that
is because of the war especially.

     MR. GRAHAM: **Yes.** You must remember the Radiator
Company is supposedly in a period of great demand for housing
this year, and yet its earnings have been very modest for 1946.
I think they are somewhere on the order of 60 cents a share.

     QUESTION: He said that with their problems they
wouldn't be too much concerned if the new building held back,
because they had this backlog of replacements, so his trouble is
one of production.

     MR. GRAHAM: Yes, for the time being it is production;
but I don't think they are doing business at the rate of 170
million a year at the present time. If they were, they would be
earning more money.

     QUESTION: What justification do we have in assuming
that their future sales will be any higher than they are this year
and that their earnings will be any higher? This is supposedly
a peak demand for them. It is an abnormal year, but how can we
assume that next year we won't have the same difficulties?

     MR. GRAHAM: I think that represents a certain amount of
optimism which ought on the whole be regarded as justified; because
operating conditions in 1946 are definitely transitional, and
you wouldn't assume that the problems of the company would be the
same in future years as they were bound to be this year. Of
course, a pessimist might make such an assumption; but I am
speaking now of the ordinary assumptions that a person would make.
He would assume that they would get around to production commensurate with demand, the same way as American business has always
done in the past.

     QUESTION: That 15 per cent profit margin -- they have
never seen a profit margin that large, have they?

     MR. GRAHAM: I think you are right in that. The
largest figure here was 14.2 for 1944; which doesn't really
mean much, because that is on war work, very largely, not on
building materials. In 1941 they reached 13.7 per cent.

     This study says that the 15 per cent margin is slightly
above that of '44 and '41, but they believe it is conservative,

based on the expectation that prices of plumbing and heating supply materials will be moderately higher, and based upon the fact that profit margins ordinarily expand with a larger volume.

It is true that, unless labor manages to get a greater cut than it used to, this company and many others will show larger profits during the building-boom period. Your point, however, emphasizes the fact that when you are going to cut the dollar sixty down because of the return of more normal conditions, you are going to cut it down, not only in proportion to the decrease in volume, but also with the expectation that the profit margin will go down on the smaller sales. That is why I am inclined to think that the one dollar figure for normal earnings is high. In fact, this morning I had made the calculation based upon seventy cents, which in my personal view, I would be more inclined to use. But I am giving away a bit to optimism today, in this analysis of American Radiator.

QUESTION: That reasoning applies to a large, well-entrenched company. What are going to be the reasonings applicable to a smaller company which is constantly growing?

MR. GRAHAM: It all depends on your own judgment as to what extent the disadvantages of smallness might be offset by the opportunities for growth in that individual company. There is no priori reason to believe that a small company gives you poorer value relatively than a large company. It does involve some greater hazard, but it also gives you greater opportunities of big developments.

It seems to me that you are back pretty much to a question of personal judgment. My own inclination is not to follow through on the idea of future growth very much unless it has been justified by the past record. I mean, a future growth based solely upon the present survey of the company's situation might lead you astray; if that made you multiply the earnings by a larger amount.

Another point that is very important here is an error that we all make in Wall Street,--and that includes me,--which is to take your future earnings of a growth company at a larger figure because they are going to grow, and then multiply them by a larger multiplier, because it is a growing company. Thus you are counting your growth factor twice. That isn't necessarily fallacious if your figures are modest; but it becomes so as soon as you begin to get really optimistic in the figures. If you mark the future earnings up a lot and you mark your multiplier up a lot, you are almost bound to overvalue the possibilities of a growth company.

Any other questions about this?

I think we will pass on from the American Radiator matter

with a final statement. I believe this type of analysis is sound
in general, if it is used with good judgment, and that it would
reflect credit on analysts in the Street if they endeavored as
far as possible to evaluate companies in terms of some rather
carefully calculated projection of future earnings and a multiplier thereof.

A thing I would like to warn you against is spending a
lot of time on over-detailed analyses of the company's and the
industry's position, including counting the last bathtub that
has been or will be produced; because you get yourself into the
feeling that, since you have studied this thing so long and
gathered together so many figures, your estimates are bound to be
highly accurate. But they won't be. They are only very rough
estimates, and I think I could have given, and probably you could
have given me, these estimates in American Radiator in half an
hour, without spending perhaps the days, or even weeks, of
studying the industry, that has gone into this larger and longer
analysis.

I would like to go to one other projection, which might
occupy us for fifteen minutes, and that is the earnings of the
United States Steel Corporation. It is interesting in the way it
relates to the, current earnings of the company. I think I
mentioned to you before that in March 1945 I had the opportunity
to speak on "Financial statements from the viewpoint of the
analyst" in a course on accounting problems to lawyers in the
Practicing Law Institute. In this address I had a short section
which dealt with the analyst's technique for appraising the
future earning power of United States Steel Corporation. That,
of course, is relevant to what we are studying today. There I
made four different calculations of the earnings of U. S. Steel,
which were based upon very simple assumptions. One was 1940
dollar volume and 1940 margin. And going through the calculations,
which were rather simple, I got earnings per share of $7.30.
The second was 1940 volume and 1944 margin. There the earnings
would be only two dollars and twenty cents, the reason being that
the profit margin had declined from 14 per cent in 1940 to 7.2
per cent in 1944.

In assumption No. 3, which was an optimistic one, I
took 1940 volume plus 25 per cent and the 1940 margin. There I
got sales of a billion four hundred million, earnings of 196
million before taxes, and a balance for the common of 90 million --
or $10.40 per share.

Finally, we have the 1940 volume plus 25 per cent and
the 1944 margin, which you remember was only half as good as
the 1940. There we get earnings as low as $3.70 per share.

The striking thing about these calculations is that
they range over such a wide area, from two dollars and twenty
cents to ten dollars and forty cents. But to some extent, I

think, they are all admissible. It is quite possible that you
could see earnings at any one of these figures for United States
Steel in the future -- or even see all of them in different years.
You might even see any of them become a so-called normal earnings
level, though that isn't so likely.

One of the interesting things that I wish to bring
out this evening is that recently the third quarter earnings for
this year of United States Steel were published; and if you
multiply them by four, here is what you get. You get sales of
$1,676 million; operating profit of 12 per cent, 196 million;
balance for common, 92 million; per share, ten dollars and
sixty cents.

Thus you find that the Steel Corporation earned in the
third quarter of this year almost exactly the rate which was
projected a year or so ago as its best likely earnings for
the future. Actually, the sales were at a higher rate than the
25 per cent above 1940 volume, but the profit margin, instead
of being 15 per cent, was down to 12 per cent.

I think that you would all agree with me that what we
have seen in the third quarter of 1946--and what we see in our
third estimate--is simply the earning power of United States
Steel Corporation under very favorable conditions, and those
favorable conditions would probably not be normal and not
continue over a period of years. The stock market at this
stage of the game is showing enough prudence not to treat the third
quarter earnings of United States Steel Corporation as a mark of
permanent earning power.

In the valuation that I made for the Institute I said
that, while the potential earnings of U. S. Stocl could vary
over this very wide range, the probabilities were that they would
tend to center somewhere around the middle of the range. They
would be somewhere around six dollars a share, on an average, as
near as we could see. I hazarded the view that the valuation of
the Steel Corporation stock would probably be made at a multiplier
of about twelve and a half, which would give you around $75 a
share for the stock. So in the case of U. S. Steel we have one
important issue in which a security analyst and todays stock
market seems to agree on the proper valuation of the shares.

As for the multiplier of twelve and a half, while it
is not a high multiplier to use for a large corporation like
United States Steel Corporation, I think you would not be
justified in using any larger one, because the Steel Corporation's
record has been not at all attractive from the standpoint of
the investor.

I would like to pause now for some questions as to this
method of projection of earnings of the Steel Corporation, if
you have any.

QUESTION: Do you take 1940 for most companies as a normal year, or do you just take United States Steel for a special reason?

MR. GRAHAM: My own inclination is to use 1940 as a kind of average expectation for the physical volume for the postwar period, unless you have some reason to think that full employment policies are going to be successful in the future, about which I have some skepticism of my own. That 1940 volume and sales results would be regarded as rather unsatisfactory for most companies, I think, in relation to the values that the market put on them earlier this year. But I think it is safer to start with 1940 and to increase that only on the basis of some knowledge as to the company's affairs which would justify your increasing it.

Remember, however, that 1940 was the figure for physical volume that I had in mind; but when you are speaking of dollar volume, you must allow for a fairly considerable marking up, because the future price level will probably be considerably higher than 1940. For that reason I am inclined to think that you would start on a dollar level probably forty or fifty per cent higher than 1940 for the typical company, but not in terms of physical units.

Are there other questions about that matter?

I want to say finally on this question that an elaborate forecasting technique has been developed in recent years on the amount of dollar business and physical volumes that would be done in various industries at certain levels of employment, or certain levels of gross national product. The Committee for Economic Development has gotten out studies of that kind which gives you estimates of the industry totals under full employment conditions, and the same has been done by the Department of Commerce. Those of you who want to go into that aspect of analysis should start pretty much with these forecasts, and accept them or reject them as far as your own judgment is concerned. If you accept them, then build your forecast of the individual company's sales in relation to the industry totals which you are starting with. You may make three different estimates,--as is now done sometimes-- based upon full employment, moderate unemployment, and considerable employment; and make your estimate of sales accordingly. That is the new technique, and I think you will find it interesting as applied to security analysis.

END OF LECTURE NO. 5

******

CURRENT PROBLEMS
IN SECURITY ANALYSIS

BY

BENJAMIN GRAHAM

Chairman of Security Analysis Department, New York Institute of Finance
Co-author, "Security Analysis" by Graham & Dodd

Transcripts of Lectures
September, 1946 — February, 1947

PART II

Martino Publishing
Mansfield Centre, CT
2010

Martino Publishing
P.O. Box 373,
Mansfield Centre, CT 06250 USA

www.martinopublishing.com

ISBN 1-57898-955-8

© 2010 *Martino Publishing*

Cover design by T. Matarazzo

Printed in the United States of America On 100% Acid-Free Paper

CURRENT PROBLEMS
IN SECURITY ANALYSIS

BY

BENJAMIN GRAHAM

Chairman of Security Analysis Department, New York Institute of Finance
Co-author, "Security Analysis" by Graham & Dodd

Transcripts of Lectures
September, 1946 — February, 1947

PART II

NEW YORK INSTITUTE OF FINANCE
Publishing Division
20 BROAD STREET   NEW YORK 5, N. Y.

NEW YORK INSTITUTE OF FINANCE
20 Broad Street New York City

Transcripts of Lectures
"CURRENT PROBLEMS IN SECURITY ANALYSIS"

BY

BENJAMIN GRAHAM

PART II
Lectures 6 thru 10

WARNING

The following transcripts of Mr. Graham's
lectures on "Current Problems in Security Analysis" contain references to specific companies
and securities. These references are for illustrative purposes only, and no attempt has been
made to provide all the facts pertinent to a
thorough analysis. Any mention of securities is
not to be construed as a suggestion to invest or
speculate in same.

Neither the New York Institute of Finance
nor Mr. Graham assume any responsibility for loss
resulting from action taken because of any statement contained in these lecture transcripts.

ALBERT P. SQUIER, DIRECTOR
NEW YORK INSTITUTE OF FINANCE

Price - ▓▓▓ per set of transcripts of ten lectures.
$5.00

NEW YORK INSTITUTE OF FINANCE
Publishing Division
20 Broad Street   New York 5, N.Y.

Lecture No. 6   December 17, 1946

CURRENT PROBLEMS IN SECURITY ANALYSIS

By
Benjamin Graham
****

MR. GRAHAM: I am sure a number of you have questions in your mind as to the proper basis for estimating sales in future years, in relation to pre-war exhibits. I have a question here from one of the students on the subject. It is my purpose this evening to go into that matter at greater length and to attempt to cover it not from the standpoint of an individual company, as we did in the case of American Radiator at the last session, and United State Steel to a smaller extent, but rather to survey the question from a broader approach.

It would seem best to consider first the question of the sales and earnings of corporations generally; then to consider a group of standard securities, and then finally to consider the application of our group results to individual companies.

The first thing that I want to make clear in any attempt to obtain a view as to future earnings, either in general or in particular, is that the analyst is not really trying to look into the crystal ball and come out with the correct answer for the period of time that he is forecasting. What he is really trying to do is to determine how the analyst should act and think--that is, how far he can go in logical thinking with respect to the always enigmatic future.

I don't believe any of us have the pretention of believing that by being very good analysts, or by going through very elaborate computations, we can be pretty sure of the correctness of our results. The only thing that we can be pretty sure of, perhaps, is that we are acting reasonably and intelligently. And if we are wrong, as we are likely to be, at least we have been intelligently wrong and not unintelligently wrong (laughter).

If we try that approach, the logical place to start, I should think, would be the experience before and after World War I. Parenthetically, I may say that as time goes on, and as we get a better perspective of the period that we are living through, the resemblance between the conditions surrounding World War I and those surrounding World War II in the economic sphere appear to grow greater than they were at first. I think earlier in the war we were more impressed by the difference in conditions. Today most

economists, I believe, are more likely to be impressed by the
resemblances.

We have quite a bit of data on general conditions in
World War I, before and after, and they might yield us some idea
as to the probabilities of general average conditions after World
War II. The first thing we start with is the national income in
dollar figures. In the three years ended 1913, that averaged
about 30 billion dollars, according to the best estimates that we
have -- there are differences between different estimates. For
the five years, 1919-23, the average was about 62 billion dollars.
That five years is a period which would interest us most at present,
because it would correspond to the period that I think our chief
interest is likely to lie in now -- the five years, 1946-50.

Between 1913 and 1920, the cost of living advanced 66
per cent and wholesale prices advanced about 44 per cent. If we
compare September 1946 figures, the latest that I have, with the
pre-war average (1935-39) we find that the cost of living is up
46 per cent and wholesale prices are up 54 per cent. The figures
are not very different, but they are reversed. You will notice
that in World War I the cost of living went up more than wholesale
prices. So far in World War II the opposite has been true. You
may be interested in the reason for that, and it is pretty clear
in the detailed figures: it lies in rents. Rents nearly doubled
between 1913 and 1920 -- well, it is more exact to say they were
up about 75 per cent. Between 1940 and September 1946 they were
up only about five per cent. And it was the rent factor, I think,
that was responsible after the last war for the big rise in the
cost of living compared with wholesale prices.

Thus you see some pretty impressive similarities in the
general price structure as it appears today, compared with the
experience after World War I; and that might lead us to make some
estimates as to the averages for 1946-50--at least based upon
former experience. We might assume an increase of about 40 per
cent in physical volume and about 50 per cent in prices for that
period, and thus end up with an assumed national income of about
100 per cent more than it was in 1940.

It may be interesting to remark that, while   an
increase in dollar income of 100 per cent is very large, it is not
as large as the full employment projections would require; because
the physical increase of 40 per cent would not be sufficient to
give us full employment in the post-war period, if productivity
develops as has been forecast. There is some doubt as to whether
productivity will develop that way now, because you are familiar
with the complaints that we are not as productive in this year
(1946) as we should be. But the fact that a dollar income of 100
per cent more than 1940 might still give us considerable unemployment would, I think, be an added reason for believing that such a
projection, large as it seems, is not unreasonable for the five-
year average.

That would seem to be a very encouraging figure to start with, with respect to the volume of business, and therefore perhaps the earnings, after the war. However, when we go back again to World War I experience and try to relate the 100 per cent increase in dollar national income to the behavior of corporate earnings, we find that the results are by no means so encouraging. And that, I think, is a matter of some importance.

EARNINGS BEFORE AND AFTER WORLD WAR I.

A

	1911	1912	1913	1919	1920	1921	1922	1923
Dow-Jones Unit	7.86	8.69	7.81	13.77	6.74	0.0	8.20	11.38

(Old List - Av. $8.12)   (New List - Av. $8.00)

B Per Share Figures

	1911	1912	1913	1919	1920	1921	1922	1923
Amer. Sugar	9.60	7.80	d0.10	13.90	d23.78	d11.80	12.01	1.92
Amer. Smalt. & R.	9.12	10.09	7.45	2.22	3.99	d0.40	3.28	8.84
Amer. Car & Fdry.	2.46	4.09	d0.10	32.24	27.67	21.50	14.94	13.71
Central Leather	d5.20	8.58	5.18	30.18	d63.80	d36.58	d4.57	d24.31
Nat. Lead	3.59	3.81	3.64	14.17	14.67	8.59	15.60	17.38
U. S. Steel	5.90	5.70	11.00	10.10	16.60	2.20	2.80	16.40

C   Earned in $ for Preferred and Common (000 omitted).

	1911	1912	1913	1919	1920	1921	1922	1923
Amer. Beet Sugar	15.86	8.81	4.12	24.25	1.33	d36.34	8.89	15.16
Amer. Radiator	13.12	16.96	20.81	30.36	33.18	31.68	60.64	109.69
Amer. Loco.	18.67	55.85	20.76	94.94	21.17	50.84	11.00	123.76
Gen. Elec.	105.60	125.80	130.00	250.70	221.30	212.60	262.30	328.70
Republic I & S.	24.23	16.73	31.01	21.41	76.17	d56.65	4.18	62.52
Studebaker	20.50	25.98	19.05	93.12	98.22	104.10	180.86	183.42
Texas Corp.	22.03	66.63	61.85	136.71	310.89	92.86	265.89	81.97
Utah Copper	62.37	84.49	85.13	82.52	49.24	d20.58	16.88	104.72

(Referring to blackboard) Down here where you can't see it, we have the Dow-Jones Industrial Average earnings for the three years ended 1913, which averaged about $8.12. And then we have them for the five post-war years from 1919 to 1923, and they unfortunately averaged only $8.00. The comparison is not as good as it should be, because the list before 1914 was very different from the list after 1914, and there is not the degree of continuity that you should have.

In all probability, the typical company did show some increase in its earnings for the period ending 1923, as compared with the period before the war. But on the whole the increase was not phenomenal. That is sure. And furthermore there were a very considerable number of decreases to balance the large increases. That is shown by the detailed comparisons which we have here on the board. You will notice that there were many losses shown during the period 1919-23. A company like Central Leather had predominant losses through that period, and a number of the other companies had some losses.

In a study of fourteen companies which I made--mainly those that appeared in the Dow-Jones Average, either before or after 1914--I found that seven of them showed larger earnings in the post-war period than before the war, six of them showed lower average earnings, and one of them was even. That one, incidentally, was United States Steel, which had widely fluctuating earnings in the period after the war, but which averaged in those five years the same figure as it did in the preceding three.

Those results were not as satisfactory as they should have been, because in that period we had the very serious depression of 1920 to 1922; and the effect of depressed conditions was to reduce the average earnings well below what they would have been if we had had a level period of national income. You recall that the figure of 62 billion dollars, which I gave you, was an average national income for the five years. But there were rather wide fluctuations from year to year, and the effect on earnings as a whole was bad. You do not gain as much from periods of unusual prosperity as you lose in periods of depression when you are in business. That is almost an axiom.

If you are not pessimistic about the future, and believe that we will be able to avoid the more serious kind of primary post-war depression, such as we had in 1921-22, you might have reason to expect somewhat better earnings, perhaps substantially better earnings in the five years 1946-50, than we had in the years prior to the war.

I would like to put down a type of calculation that might be reasonable on the basis of that assumption, and see where we get. Suppose you take a typical company, which in 1940 had sales of $100 and profit margin of 10 per cent, less a tax of 18 per cent, and thus had left $8.20 net.

Let us assume that in the post-war period the sales correspond to our expectation of national income, and go up to $200. This we call average post-war. The first question is what is reasonable with regard to profit margin? Normally you think profit margin increases as sales increase, and that would be so if you had a sudden change. I think it would be both reasonable and conservative to assume that the profit margins will decrease in this post-war period, because of the strongly entrenched position of Labor and its determined effort to obtain a large part of the gains through higher wages or through lower prices. If we assume that the profit margin will generally decrease by 20 per cent, it would here be reduced to 8 per cent. That would give you $16 of earnings before taxes. If you assume tax rates of 35%, which I think is a little optimistic, for the next five years (we now have 38%) the tax will amount to $5.60. Thus the balance after taxes is $10.40, which is an increase of a little more than 25 per cent in net earnings.

Incidentally, this calculation does not depend upon the assumption of a profit margin of 10 per cent to begin with, but depends on the assumption that whatever the profit margin was, it would be reduced by 20 per cent in the post-war period. And if that is so, you would have an increase of 25 per cent in your net earnings corresponding to an increase of 100 per cent in your sales.

Suppose I pause at this time for questions with regard to that calculation. I am going to assume, for the future, that this would be the type of central figure that an analyst would be likely to use or start with in making his projections.

You have a question?

QUESTION: I would like to know why you use the year 1940 instead of, let us say, the average of 1936-40?

MR. GRAHAM: That is a perfectly good question. I use 1940 simply for convenience because the figure of sales that I had in mind, or national income, was related in the first instance to the 1940 figure. If you took the average of 1936-40, you would have a slightly lower figure, but you would have a slightly larger increase in sales, in your projection of increased physical volume and increased prices. Your question is really more relevant to the matter of an individual company, where you might have very substantial differences between the 1940 average and the 1936-40 average. For a group of companies, such as the Dow-Jones list, the difference is not particularly important.

QUESTION: Wouldn't it give you lower earnings in the long run?

MR. GRAHAM: It would give you somewhat lower earnings to begin with; but if you stepped up your expected increase in sales correspondingly by a small amount, you would end up with the same figure. I think that perhaps the average of 1936-40 might have been on the order of 90, or more like 95, as against the 100 in sales in 1940, so our increase would be 110 per cent rather than 100 per cent.

Were there other questions about that?

I might add it is easier to use the 1940 figure than an average, because you don't have to do as much work. But that I would not consider to be an adequate reply to your question (laughter).

Let us now apply that calculation to a group of stocks such as the present Dow-Jones Industrial average. We find that the Dow-Jones Average earned $10.85 in 1940 per unit. If you add 25 per cent to that you would get approximately $13.60 as the projected average earnings of the Dow-Jones unit for 1946-50. At this point you might inquire why I am now speaking of projected

earnings of $13.60, when in the valuation that I used in the
"Chronicle" article I started from or accepted the past earnings
of about $10, which I said was an apparent central point to which
the Dow-Jones earnings always seemed to return whenever they
departed from it.

I think that there is a sound reason for using a different
figure in this discussion. In the first place, when the article
was written in October 1945, the price level was under very good
control, and it was not particularly sound perhaps to project a
substantial increase in the price level for the post-war period
at that time. It looks now as if our price experience will be
roughly similar to what we had after World War I; and it also looks
as if the plateau of prices, which we will have after the up and
down adjustments have been completed during the early years, will
in some wise correspond to our post-war experience back in 1923--
namely, an increase of about 50 per cent in the price level.

On that basis there might be reason to believe that the
future earnings of the Dow-Jones Industrial Average, representing
strong companies on the whole, should reflect to some extent the
combination of both a much higher price level and an expected
increase in physical volume. And I believe that one would be more
reasonable in making that assumption than in thinking that the
historic $10 must necessarily continue just because you have had
it so often in the past.

QUESTION: Why do you expect an increase of
physical volume?

MR. GRAHAM: Our economic history has indicated that
physical volume does increase over the years. I think there will
be very considerable reasons for special endeavor to create an
increase in physical volume and for at least partially succeeding
in that endeavor. Where tremendous emphasis is now placed upon full
employment in the future, the necessity for having it, it seems
to me, will entail all sections of the economy bending their efforts
to getting a degree of physical volume that will come close to it.

QUESTION: What is the likelihood of success?

MR. GRAHAM: I think the success will be only
partial; that is my personal opinion. But it will be partial at
least.

QUESTION: I just wondered how you measure that
partial success.

MR. GRAHAM: One way of course of doing it was to
assume that the post-war experience of World War I will more or
less repeat itself. The increase in volume was on the order of
40 per cent there, when you compare your 31 billion with your
62 billion and allow for your price rise of roughly 50 per cent.

Of course, it is a very arbitrary assumption that we shall have
the same experience, but it is not as improbable as it may sound
to some.

          QUESTION: Would you say that the increase of
25 per cent in net earnings was on an optimistic basis, or is that
what you think is probable?

          MR. GRAHAM: I think that it is optimistic in the
sense that you are not expecting the average earnings experience
to be badly affected by a depression period during the next five
years. You will remember that I pointed out that the experience
in 1919-23 included a depression period even in the figures which
gave you the 100 per cent average increase in dollar national
income.

          I want to say, though, that just because we are raising
our estimate of Dow-Jones earnings to $13.60, based largely upon
the price increase, we should also recognize an extra risk of a
depression period supervening. For when you have a change in
the picture represented by a wide price advance, you are undoubtedly introducing certain factors of vulnerability in the
position of the economy as a whole. There are inventory risks;
the price advance will probably go too far, as it always does
(just as it does in the stock market); and it will be succeeded
by a price decline, and by inventory losses.

          During the period 1920 to 1922, the major losses of
corporations were sustained on inventories. That is shown in very
graphic form by the Central Leather figures, in which you see
that they succeeded in losing $63.80 per share in 1920--although
this was peculiarly a good year as far as business volume went.
But, as it happened, it was a very bad year as far as change in
raw material prices were concerned; and that hit Central Leather
very badly. We may have something like that in the next few years.
I am not going to take the responsibility of predicting or even
guessing whether we will or not; but it is a factor to bear in mind.

          Before we pursue the implications of these possible
earnings of $13.60 for Dow-Jones any farther, I think we ought
to consider other groups of stocks besides the Dow-Jones Industrial
Average.

          The Dow-Jones is a very particular group. It has had
much more stability in earnings than others. It has shown some
resistance to increased earnings during the war as well as to
decreased earnings during depression. Let us consider a secondary
group for a moment, and I think I would like to pick out more
or less at random a secondary group which is somewhat better
than the average secondary group.

          Looking for some stocks to take, I picked eight companies
that appeared in two tables in Security Analysis, on page 689-690.

They were stocks that appeared very cheap at the end of '38 or '39; and they proved to be very cheap in actual experience. They had reasonably good earnings, and they had a wealth of current assets in relation to price. If we pick out the seven companies that were listed on the New York Stock Exchange, we have what might be called quite an attractive group of secondary stocks to compare with the Dow-Jones list.

Let me read the names of the seven companies. They are American Seating, Butler Brothers, Grand Union, International Silver, Intertype, Manhattan Shirt, and Reliance Manufacturing. Except for the last two, which are in the same industry, you would say that it was a remarkably diversified group of companies from the standpoint of operating characteristics.

Let us see about their earnings in 1940 and 1945, and the projected earnings. It happens that these seven stocks earned together $11.88 in 1940, which was very close to the Dow-Jones unit figure. That, of course, was a coincidence.

Suppose I put some figures on the blackboard which may be interesting. Here is Dow-Jones, here are seven secondary companies. The Dow-Jones list earned $10.65 in 1940; eight secondary companies $11.88. In 1945 Dow-Jones earned a little less, $10.42; the secondary companies earned $14.31. If we add 25 per cent to 1940 you would get $13.60 for Dow-Jones, and about $14 for the secondary group.

Let us take a look at market prices. The 1946 high for the Dow-Jones, as some of you probably know, is 212, and the current level is about 174. On these seven secondary companies the high was 297, for one share of each, and the current is about 200. The multiplier: Dow-Jones was selling, at its high, at about 16 times our projected earnings. The secondary companies were selling about 20 times. Currently Dow-Jones is selling about 13 times and the secondary companies about $13\frac{1}{2}$ times their projected earnings.

I have one other group of stocks to bring into the proceeding, which might be called tertiary stocks, or third grade stocks; and they would represent the new offerings of common stocks of which we have been afflicted with such a large quantity. I didn't want the bother of taking a lot of time to make up an index for a large group of these companies, because the showing is similar in a melancholy way for almost all the stocks which you might look at. But I just picked out four of them which I happened to have under my hand, including one that was offered today. Portis Style Industries, (men's caps); the Northern Engineering and Manufacturing, which I referred to in my first lecture; Glen Industries, a women's dress company; and Glen Gary Shale Brick, a construction company. If you add those four companies up you would find that you would have paid $34 for one share of each; that you would have had combined earnings of 70 cents in 1940, and $1.09 in 1945.

The probabilities are that tertiary companies in general were sold to the public at between 30 and 50 times their earnings as projected by our formula--namely, 1940 earnings plus 25 per cent. And if we use the average of 1936-1940, as has been suggested, the multiplier would be far larger.

I think these figures that I have given you illustrate a situation in the current market picture which is quite unusual, and that is the fact that the leading stocks appear now, as they have appeared for quite a while, to be more reasonably priced than the secondary issues.

The probable reason for it, as I indicated some time ago, is the fact that the market has not yet discounted the results of a return of competition in sales. It may be that this competition will not return. If so, I shall be the most surprised person in this group. But just looking at the picture as it is presented in terms of our pro-forma projection of future earnings and current prices, you find that the Dow-Jones stocks at 13 times this projection would be by no means high. They would seem to be valued today on the low side.

On the other side of the picture, the secondary stocks, with the same or a slightly higher multiplier, must be regarded as being valued on the high side; because there is a real difference in the financial strength of the two groups of companies, in their respective vulnerability to adverse conditions in the future, and I think most of us would agree that a higher multiplier should be applied to the primary companies than to the secondary companies. My fight has always been in the other direction, to try to prevent people from setting too large a premium for the high-grade companies which they like. But I don't think any of us would argue that no premium is to be paid for financial strength and preeminence in the various industries.

We find, going down to the third group, that the new offerings are obviously too high from our schematic approach; and they must be too high from any common-sense viewpoint at all.

A question that has given me pause about this is the following: How would these discrepancies in value normally adjust themselves in our future experience? There are various possibilities to consider here. One is that our analysis may be wrong; that the secondary issues will do better in comparison with the Dow-Jones list in the future than they did before the war; and that the Dow-Jones list is not entitled to a better valuation in terms of, say, its 1940 performance.

The second possibility is that there is a further readjustment period ahead in the general market. And when we say "a further readjustment period," you will understand that we are using a euphemistic expression for a further decline in prices. During that readjustment period and its sequel of recovery there

will be plenty of opportunity for more correct price relationships
to establish themselves between first-line and second-line
companies.

Incidentally, that type of readjustment has already showed
itself in the experience we have had since last May; because, as
you see, the secondary companies lost about one-third of their
price and the Dow-Jones list lost considerably less, more like 18
per cent of their price.

It may be that more of that experience will have to be
gone through in order to arrive at a correct price relationship
between the various groups.

There is, of course, a third possibility, which is more
attractive from all angles, and that is that there will be a
gradual set of market changes over the next few years, during which
the Dow-Jones list will slowly outstrip the secondary group,
starting from the present relationship. You will have to form your
own ideas as to which of these three possibilities is the more
likely one. As you see, there is plenty of room for individual
judgment and individual errors in forecasting future earnings of
groups, and in forecasting their basic values, even if we all
start with the same apparatus of analysis.

Let me pause at this point and see how many questions
have formed themselves in your mind on this matter.

We have gone into two aspects: one is a projection of
group earnings and secondly a very rough evaluation of those
earnings in terms of a proper price level, distinguishing between
different groups.

I would like now to support what I said about the value
of the Dow-Jones list, and also to add a word of caution about it
by reference to the experience in that list after World War I.

The high price of the Dow-Jones stocks in 1919 was a
little under 120, and that was based upon a good deal of market
enthusiasm, which turned out to have been misguided in good part--
as shown by the fall to 64 in 1921. Nevertheless, that high price
was not really too high in relation to the longer term future of
the Dow-Jones group from the standpoints both of earnings and of
price.

In 1923, which corresponds roughly to the 1950 year that
we are thinking of, the earnings on the Dow-Jones unit were
$11.36, and that certainly justified the high price of 120 in 1919.
By the end of 1924 that price was re-established in the market, and
instead of being a high price it was just about the beginning of
a long and ill-fated bull market which went on for five years and
ended at the level of 381.

I am more and more impressed with the possibilities of history's repeating itself on many different counts. You don't get very far in Wall Street with the simple, convenient conclusion that a given level of prices is not too high. It may be that a great deal of water will have to go over the dam before a conclusion of that kind works itself out in terms of satisfactory experience. That is why in this course we have tried to emphasize as much as possible the obtaining of specific insurance against adverse developments by trying to buy securities that are not only not too high but that, on the basis of analysis, appear to be very much too low. If you do that, you always have the right to say to yourself that you are out of the security market, and you are an owner of part of a company on attractive terms. It is a great advantage to be able to put yourself in that psychological frame of mind when the market is not going the way you would like.

The experience of World War I, and at many other times, would seem to indicate that the buying of securities at a level which may be fully justified by your analysis will not at all guarantee that you will get immediate profits, or that you will not suffer some rather substantial market losses for a while. That is the warning I think it is necessary to sound at this time, in connection with the preceding conclusion that the level of prices for the Dow-Jones Average today would seem to be more on the low side than it would be on the high side.

Are there any questions about that conclusion and the warning that goes with it?

QUESTION: I wondered if the cash position of the market -- you know, the elimination of   margins -- has anything to do with the trend in the market, so you could make a comparison there.

MR. GRAHAM: You are speaking now, of course, of the possible or probable market action in this post-war period as compared with the last one?

QUESTION: Yes. If that has any effect on it.

MR. GRAHAM: That is a matter of opinion, and I think it is also a controversial matter. My own impression is this: that the chief effect of requiring cash purchases has been to reduce the amount of trading which is associated with any given price change, both up or down. But it has not had any noticeable effect upon the amplitude or width of the price changes. The market went up in the past few years in a good old-fashioned bull-market way and has shown some tendency to go down in a similar fashion, on a cash basis. I see no particular reason to believe that the prospect of fairly large fluctuations in prices will be any different on a cash basis than they would be on a margin basis. It used to be argued that when you traded on a ten per cent margin, it only took a ten per cent decline or less in prices to force the lightweights out of the market, i.e. to have the "necessary corrections." Now when you have a cash market it may be necessary to have very wide declines in order that justice should be done and the people who don't belong in the market should be compelled to get out. That is a very cynical expression, I know, but I think it has a certain germ of truth in it.

QUESTION: I notice that on your figures, in 1919 the Dow-Jones Average was 13.77.

MR. GRAHAM: Those were the earnings.

QUESTION: In 1929, the average reached 25 or 30 times the 1919 earnings.

MR. GRAHAM: Yes.

QUESTION: Why can't you say that there is a possibility that during the ensuing market, the price level might now reach, say, 25 times the 1945 earnings?

MR. GRAHAM: Your comparison goes far ahead from 1919 to 1929, which is ten years later.

QUESTION: In other words, in the ensuing bull market, after World War I, the price average reached over 25 times the earnings of 1919, which was the year after the war.

MR. GRAHAM: Yes.

QUESTION: At the present time, I mean the 1945 earnings are $10.42. Isn't it possible that in the next bull market, if there should be one, it might not get to 25 times that?

MR. GRAHAM: Oh, yes, I think the implication of what I have been saying through this hour has been exactly that. As far as you can judge probabilities, they would warrant the belief that not only would the high prices carry you to a figure such as you mentioned, but even the central price would be above our current price. But my warning, and I must repeat it, was that when you go back to World War I experience for that encouragement, you must also go back to World War I experience for the intervening hazards, and they were very great. For, as you know, you had no earnings in the year 1921, and you had a price as low as 64 for the Dow-Jones average, about half of the top price of 1919. That, I think, is the real hurdle that faces people who are optimistic today about the general relationship of future prices and future earnings.

QUESTION: Would you feel that a much higher multiplier should be put on Dow-Jones in the post-war period than after World War I, in view of the fact that long-term interest rates are now almost half, compared with the post-war period after the first world war?

MR. GRAHAM: Oh, yes. That is why I believe that
the high price in '46 of 212, which is, say, 16 times these
projected earnings, is not a particularly high price in terms of
valuation theory, because a multiplier related to the low interest
rates could readily be more than sixteen times. However, I am
inclined to mark down the multiplier somewhat from the indicated
twenty times, because I believe there is an underlying drag on
profits that goes along with low interest rates. Hence the general
effect of lowered interest rates will make itself shown in some way
or other in lower profits. The two have an economic connection.
But it may be argued that this has been allowed for in assuming
an eight per cent profit margin in 1946-50 instead of 10 per cent.

Of course, we have no real point of disagreement here,
because I am inclined to say that the multiplier of 16 could not
be regarded as a high multiplier in the light of current and
prospective interest rates and the character of the companies
with which you are dealing here.

QUESTION: Shouldn't you take into consideration the
average multiplier of companies where the price earnings ratio
was, say, 20, consistently, or even more? They rarely go down to
sixteen. Take a stock like General Electric. That always sells
at a very high multiplier, doesn't it?

MR. GRAHAM: Yes. We have an advantage here in
dealing with a large group of stocks, from which we get a resultant
of a number of different factors. While the group as a whole is
a high-grade group, there are considerable variations in it.
General Electric appears in this group and its multiplier would
be fully 20, or more. On the other hand, United States Steel
also appears in the group, and I am inclined to think that its
multiplier would be under 16; in fact, in the discussion last week
I mentioned 12½ for United States Steel.

QUESTION: What I meant is when you take the
individual stocks that are in the group   --such as General
Electric or United States Steel--shouldn't you use a higher or a
lower multiplier in proportion to the average multiplier at which
the stock has been selling over a period of years?

MR. GRAHAM: Oh, yes. Nothing that has been said
hitherto would conflict with that suggestion. In fact, there
has been nothing said so far that has had any bearing on that
question; because we have designedly confined ourselves to
dealing with a group of securities. Our next section was to deal
with the individual securities, at least in a somewhat sketchy way.

Are there any other questions about these group
valuations?

There are great advantages in dealing with a group
valuation, because you are more likely to be nearly accurate,

I am sure, when you are considering a number of components together--
in which your errors are likely to cancel out--than when you are
concentrating on an individual component and may go very wide of
the mark in that one.

Furthermore, there is nothing to prevent the investor from
dealing with his own investment problems on a group basis. There
is nothing to prevent the investor from actually buying the Dow-
Jones Industrial Average, though I never heard of anybody doing it.
It seems to me it would make a great deal of sense if he did.

When we talk about buying bargain issues, for example,
the emphasis on group operation becomes even greater, because you
then get into what could practically be known as an insurance type
of operation. Here you have an edge, apparently, on each individual
company. That advantage may conceivably disappear or not be
realized in the individual case; but if you are any good at all
as an analyst you ought to realize that advantage in the group.
And so I have had a great partiality for group operations and group
analysis. I must say, however, that you gentlemen, as functioning
security analysts, advisers to the multitude, and so on, are unable
to obtain that advantage in all the work you do. For I am sure
you are compelled to reach rather definite conclusions about
individual companies, and can't hide them in a group result.

Since I have one more minute, I would like to make an
observation about the Dow-Jones list, viz: These earnings of the
Dow-Jones list that you may have had occasion to study, and which
appeared in the article I gave you, are somewhat deceptive because
they are not the same stocks in each year. Actually, they would be
correct enough if the investor did what the Dow-Jones adjusters
did, and sold out certain securities and replaced them with others
from time to time. But there is a rather considerable amount of
hindsight in the choice of the stocks that go into the list, and the
result is somewhat paradoxical. The effect is to make the earnings
trend appear poorer than it would have been in the past, if you had
had the present list all the way through. But it is by no means
certain that you would make a profit by switching out of the poorer
appearing companies into the better ones, the way the Dow-Jones list
has done. The reason is that when the companies appear to be
better and seem to belong in a high-grade investment list, rather
than other ones that appear worse, the market price of the good
ones is considerably higher. Thus when you switch from the "bad"
stocks into the "good" ones, you sell at a low price and you buy
at a high price. It is very easy to show that one of the chief
reasons why the Dow-Jones list did not act as well as the 354
stocks in the Standard Statistics industrial list between 1929
and 1946 is that they made so many switches to improve its
character--especially in 1932--that they lost a good part of the
market price advance from that year.

Lecture No. 7   January 14, 1947.

CURRENT PROBLEMS IN SECURITY ANALYSIS

By
Benjamin Graham
****

MR. GRAHAM: Good evening. You have all had a
month's rest since the last lecture. I hope you had a pleasant
vacation during that period and you are now ready to absorb some
more punishment.

If you recall as far back as the last lecture, we dealt
there mainly with the prospective earning power of the Dow-Jones
list considered as a unit, and with its prospective central market
value.

You might now ask the question: What about the earnings
of the individual components of the Dow-Jones list? How would one
go about evaluating them, and what results would you get?

As it happens, that job was done--at least from the
standpoint of expected earning power--in an article that appeared
in the Analyst Journal in July 1945. It is called "Estimating
Earnings of an Active Post-War Year," and it is by Charles J.
Collins. There he gives his estimate of the postwar earnings of
all the companies in the Dow-Jones unit, together with the sum of
these earnings.

His total figure varies from $15.96 to $17.58 per unit.
You may recall that my rather rough calculation gave a figure of
$13.60, and it may thus appear that my figure is rather definitely
lower than Collins'. Actually that may not be true, because
Collins identifies his earnings as those of an active postwar
year, whereas the earnings that I had used in the last lecture are
supposed to represent the average future earning power of the Dow-
Jones unit--which would include some allowance for poor years
as well as good ones.

It is interesting to note that Collins' estimates for
individual companies show considerable variation from their pre-war
earnings, say their 1940 figures. I might read off a few to you
to show how different are his expectations for different companies.

Here are four that show large expected increases, taking
1940 as against the future years: American Smelting, from $4.21
to $9.50; Chrysler, from $8.69 to $17.75; Johns Manville, from
$6.35 to $14.75; Goodyear, from $3.44 to $8.60.

Here are four others that show very small increases,
if any: (I am using here, the average of his range of figures)
American Tel and Tel, from $10.08 to $10.50; American Tobacco
from $5.59 to $5.90; National Distillers, from $3.28 to $3.35;
and Woolworth, from $2.48, in 1940, to $2.62 in the postwar year.

Collins does not give his method of calculation in
detail, but he does give you a description which you can follow
through fairly well.

He starts from industry sales projections which have
been made by the Committee for Economic Development of the
Department of Commerce, and he adjusts them to an expected national
income of $112 billion. That happens to be quite a conservative
figure, because the national income for the year 1946 was about
165 billion.

He does not apply the exact percentage increase in each
industry to the particular company; but he allows for its better
or poorer trend than that of the industry as a whole over the
period from 1929 to 1940. He assumes, in other words, that a
company which did better than its industry from 1929 to 1940 will
do proportionately better in the increase that is to be seen from
pre-war; and correspondingly for those that may have done worse.

From the estimated sales he then calculates net before
taxes based on pre-war ratios; he takes taxes of 40 per cent; and
that gives him his figure, with a small range that he allows for
possible adjustments.

You will recall that the profit margin that we used was
distinctly lower than the pre-war; but on the other hand we took
a considerably higher national income, and we also took a lower
expected tax.

These variations in method suggest that there is no
single way of dealing with a projection of future earnings, and
that individual judgment will have to play a considerable part.
But the variations in this technique are not likely to be as great
as the variations in the market's response to what it thinks are
the possibilities of different companies.

I would not criticize the Collins' method, except in one
respect which I think it is rather significant to consider. He
assumes that the trends shown from 1929 to 1940 will continue in
the future, and that seems a natural assumption to make. But I
would like to warn you against placing too much reliance on that
supposition.

Some years ago we made a rather intensive study on the
subject of whether earnings trends did or did not continue. We
tried to find out what happened to companies showing an improvement
in their earnings from 1926 to 1930, comparing them further with

1935.; and also those that had failed to show improvement in the period. We found that there were at least as many cases of companies failing to maintain their trend as there were of those that did continue their trends. And that is a very vital consideration in all future projections.

As a matter of fact, Collins himself says that, when he accepts the trends, in some cases he finds he gets such large earnings that he felt constrained to reduce them in the interests of conservatism; and I imagine he was probably right.

Have you any questions to ask about this method applied to individual stocks, as I have given it to you in a sketchy fashion?

It would not do any harm for you to read this article. I know the magazine is available in many brokerage offices.

QUESTION: Could we have the name of it?

MR. GRAHAM: It is "The Analyst Journal," which is the publication of the New York Society of Security Analysts.* I imagine there are many members here. The issue is July 1945.

Any other questions on the subject?

Now, I would like to finish this portion of our general investigation by applying the method of appraisal to a secondary company, one of distinctly smaller size--just, of course, as an example of our technique.

I selected a company more or less at random, Barker Bros. Then, when I found myself going along in the work, it seemed almost inevitable that I would try to compare it with some other company in order to reach some more definite conclusions.

But let us start with Barker Brothers on the basis of a calculation of its future earning power. What I have on the blackboard is not really a presentation from that point of view, but a presentation from the point of view of the comparison of two stocks. Let us, however, speak first about the projected future earnings of Barker.

---

* Quarterly publication. Subscription price for four issues is $3; single copies are $1. Checks should be drawn to the order of New York Society of Security Analysts and forwarded to Oscar Miller, Business Manager, 44 Wall Street, New York 5, New York.

T A B L E

	Barker Bros.	Mandel Bros.
Price 12/31/46	25-3/4	12-3/4
# common shares	356,000	300,000
Market value of common	9,000,000	3,825,000
" " " preferred	2,250,000	-----
Total capitalization	11,250,000	3,825,000

	Average 1941-45	Average 1936-40	Average 1941-45	Average 1936-40
Sales (millions)	$15.4	$12.7	$27.4	$18.6
Net for common	407,000	222,000	456,000	298,000
Earned per share	1.14	.62	1.52	.99
Market price	6-3/4	5-5/8	8-7/8	6-7/8

(Per share figures are adjusted for split-up and stock dividend.)

(000 omitted)

Balance Sheet	12/31/45	9/30/46	1/31/46
Net Current Assets	4874	5714	5018
Other Assets (net)	3018	2917	1097
Total for pfd and common	7892	8631	6115

	9 months to September 30		6 months to July 31	
	1946	1945	1946	1945
Sales	16,100,000	11,600,000	16,300,000	12,400,000
Net before taxes	2,306,000	1,334,000	824,000	560,000
Net after taxes	1,348,000	403,000	435,000	207,000
Earned per share	$3.57	$0.87	$1.45	$0.69

- -

Taking the sales of Barker Brothers, in 1940 they amounted to $12.6 million, which is about its average for five years. The average during the war period was $15.4 million. We might assume sales for the postwar period as high as $20 million.

The net earnings in 1940, before tax, were 5.3 per cent of sales, and that was better than its average for the pre-war period. I am inclined to think that if we accepted a 5.3 per cent figure, we would be fairly optimistic, considering the competition and the lower profit margins that are likely to develop in the postwar period. We should also allow for the opposite fact that, as sales go up, there is a tendency for the profit margin to rise--at least immediately. But peculiarly enough, companies always seem to adjust themselves to a larger amount of business ultimately in such a way that they don't make any more profit per dollar on the larger business than they used to make on the smaller.

If we take a 5.3 per cent margin, we would have earnings of $1,060,000 before taxes, $689,000 after taxes, and $1.70 per share on the stock.

The next question is what multiplier should we apply to expected future earnings of $1.70 for this company. Our suggestion has been that the shares of smaller companies occupying a secondary position and with records that are not very satisfactory when you study them over a period of years--those companies should be valued on a fairly modest basis, and I would be inclined to think that a multiplier of 12 would be as high as you would be likely to adopt. On that basis you would get a valuation of this company between 20 and 21--without any allowance for asset considerations, which for the moment I will put aside. (In fact, they are not very important).

If that method of valuation is right, it is pretty significant. For one thing, the stock closed 1946 at 25-3/4, which is 28 per cent higher than our valuation; and it sold as high as 41 last year, which is more than double our valuation. Thus the difference between our valuation and the price is here on the side of a conservative or unfavorable conclusion; whereas you will recall that when we were valuing the Dow-Jones average, we ended with a value higher than the current market price--quite a bit higher.

I think that example bears out the general statement that I made some time ago, that the secondary companies do not show up as well in our technique of analysis as do the leading companies.

In order to test that conclusion with regard to Barker, I thought I would introduce another company for the comparison-- Mandel Brothers, which is in somewhat the same type of business. Barker Brothers, as you know, has house furnishings stores in Los Angeles and other towns nearby. Mandel Brothers has a large department store in Chicago. The two businesses are not precisely the same, but they are similar. Barker Brothers has a larger degree of ownership of its buildings than Mandel Brothers has, and that is one reason why the net profit on sales for Mandel Brothers would be lower than that of Barker. But those are not really essential differences.

If we go on to the projection of Mandel's earnings and profits, we get something like this: Mandel having had sales of $18.5 million, on the average, before the war, and $27 million during the war, might well have sales of $30 million in the postwar period.

Its profit margin was very low during the pre-war years. Hence it might be correct to assume that on the 30 million volume, this company could make a somewhat better margin of profit than it did before the war. I had taken one half of the Barker Brothers pre-war margin, as my feeling of the margin Mandel should make, or else somebody should know the reason why. That would give them a margin of 2.65%, earnings of $900,000 before taxes, and $515,000 or $2.60 per share after taxes.

The striking thing about these figures is that the
Mandel Brothers projection shows earnings 50 per cent higher than
those of Barker Brothers, although Barker is selling at about twice
the price of Mandel. And correspondingly, if you were to multiply
those earnings by about twelve, you would get valuation of around
$30 a share for Mandel as compared with 20 for Barker--completely
different figures than the market prices suggest.

You will note that I have taken examples here which create
difficulties for me. They are more interesting than more conventional valuations, where the market price seems to be more or less
in line.

Before we try to reach any conclusion as to the soundness
of this valuation which gives you a so much better result for
Mandel than for Barker, let us try to trace the two companies
through, on a more or less complete statistical comparison. That
has been put on the board.

You find that Barker Brothers is selling in the market
for $11¼ million, including $2-1/4 million of preferred stock.
Mandel is selling for $3,825,000, or one-third the price of Barker.
It is interesting to see that Mandel's sales are uniformly about
50 per cent higher than Barker's.

The five-year period before the war showed average
earnings of 62 cents for Barker and 99 cents for Mandel. The
average market price before the war was 5-5/8 for Barker, (allowing
for a hundred per cent stock dividend) and 6-7/8 for Mandel
(allowing for a 20 per cent stock dividend).

During the war period the earnings for Barker averaged
$1.14, and those for Mandel $1.52. The average price of Barker
was 6-3/4, and that for Mandel 8-7/8.

So far we seem to have our relative valuations justified
by both average sales, average earnings, and average market prices.

Let us go on to the asset picture. If you compare them
at about the same date, the end of 1945 roughly, Barker had $7.9
million of assets for $11-1/4 million of market price. Mandel
had $6.1 million of assets for $3,825,000 of market price. Hence,
on the asset picture--and that would apply also to current assets,
considered separately--the Mandel valuation seems justified, and
the market prices seem out of line.

Let us go on, however, to the developments in 1946, so
far as known. There, undoubtedly, we are going to find something
that will explain the market's action. We have nine months'
results for Barker and six months' results for Mandel. The sales
figures happen to be about the same in nine months for Barker as in
six months for Mandel.

Barker's sales for nine months of 1945 were $11.6 million, and they rose to $16.1 million, a somewhat greater expansion for Barker than for Mandel.

The earnings before taxes rose somewhat more, proportionately, for Barker than they did for Mandel. Mandel's increased somewhat less than fifty per cent; Barker's about 80 per cent. The net after taxes more than tripled for Barker, and somewhat more than doubled for Mandel. We find that in 9 months Barker earned $3.57 a share, and Mandel showed $1.45; as against 87 cents for Barker and 69 cents for Mandel in corresponding periods the year before.

It is pretty clear that the stock market derived a great deal of comfort and perhaps enthusiasm out of the fact that in nine months Barker was able to earn as much as $3.50 a share. Its theory must have been that the price--either 40 at the high, or 25 at the end of the year--would not be out of line with earnings at that rate. Actually the earnings for the twelve months ended September 30 were about four dollars a share for Barker.

I think an analyst, looking at those figures, would have some cause for skepticism as to their dependability in the future. The profit margin of Barker was about 14 per cent in that period of time. You will notice that of Mandel was about five per cent. These are earnings before taxes. I don't believe it is in the wood for a house-furnishings company to do business on a fourteen per cent margin over a period of years in the future. And I don't believe that the Barker Brothers people themselves would expect any results of the kind. Those I would call distinctly boom results; and I believe that in this case, as so often in the market, a fundamental error is made in accepting temporary results as if they were permanent.

It may be that we are wrong in this skepticism. Something may have happened to the Barker business that has turned it around completely. I recall very well when it was a most unpopular company when it sold at considerably less than its working capital, and nobody wanted to touch it at all. Those of you who have read "Security Analysis" may remember that we used it as an example of a bona fide low-price stock when it was selling at four or five dollars a share, before the hundred per cent stock dividend.

Now we find the market's view seems to have changed completely. We have yet to see any well thought out, carefully considered explanation of why values have been so completely revolutionized in the case of a company of this sort, when the values for the highest grade companies have shown relatively small changes. I think this is a good point at which to pause for inquiry, and perhaps objection, on our analysis and comparison. I imagine some question must have occurred to you about it.

It is rather interesting to point out, in the case of Mandel, that the company is selling for $3,825,000, while its working capital is five million dollars. Thus that company is selling for less than its net current assets, whereas at a more or less corresponding date Barker was selling for close to three times its working capital.

QUESTION: You did not give us the net before taxes for the pre-war period. I conclude from the figures as you put them down that the Mandel profit margin was less than five per cent.

MR. GRAHAM: Oh, yes. You recall that my estimate was a profit margin of only 2.65% for the future, about half of Barker's for 1940.

QUESTION: These secondary companies are one thing. What would you consider a first-grade company in this particular line of business?

MR. GRAHAM: That is a little hard to say. I imagine that many department stores would rank as first-class companies in this line of business.

QUESTION: How do you compare those like Gimbels, Macy's?

MR. GRAHAM: Well, Gimbels--just as a matter of opinion--would not rank quite so high, because it was an over-capitalized company years ago, with a rather irregular record. It has improved its position a great deal: but not enough, to my mind, to warrant its being considered the best kind of company. Macy's presents a somewhat different and more complicated question. I won't try to answer it here.

QUESTION: Would it be necessary to make an investigation for the reason for that great difference in profit margin? Wouldn't it be possible to get an analysis of the sales and of the location? I mean, the type of people they do business with might have an effect upon their profit margin: and the kind of business they do might also. I understand that Barker does some interior decorating, or something like that; they have a special department.

MR. GRAHAM: Let me interrupt you, because I think you have made the point. You mustn't confuse the question of the basic difference in the character of the companies with the question of what happened in the year 1946. The basic difference in the character of the companies would presumably show itself in our analyses of five-year and ten-year results. Of course we think Barker is a better type of company in terms of what is known as "quality of merchandise" than Mandel; that is why its profit margin is higher. But that is all in the results and it explains in part why, per dollar of sales, Barker is undoubtedly worth more than Mandel. However, the fact that a company has a better store in terms of quality of merchandise doesn't necessarily mean it is a better stock; and it certainly doesn't mean that it is a better stock at any given or any imagined market price. Your distinctions have to keep these points in mind.

QUESTION: But the good will factor has something to do with it.

MR. GRAHAM: A company may get more good will, possibly, selling merchandise at low prices than selling at high prices. At one time, as you know, Macy's had a tremendous reputation on that very factor.

Your suggestion that an inquiry should be made is a perfectly valid one. The inquiry should confine itself, for practical purposes, to the developments in 1946, with an eye to finding out whether there was any basic change in the relative positions of these two companies, or whether it was merely a divergent reaction to the short-term situation. You might be disappointed with the low profit margin of Mandel in '46, as compared with Barker's, and that may need some explanation.

That, of course, is a good suggestion to make; because I haven't emphasized as much as I want to that when we take ten minutes to analyze a company, and draw conclusions therefrom, we are not suggesting that we have exhausted the analysis of the concern. As a matter of fact, these results, if they are interesting, should suggest to the analyst that he go forward and further and try to get a good deal more information about the companies than we present here.

QUESTION: Is there anything to watch for concerning a company's dealings on a cash basis as opposed to a credit basis?

MR. GRAHAM: That is something you want to look at, though the exact significance even of that factor is not too easy to see. You know that if a company does a lot of installment business it is more vulnerable to sudden changes in credit, and in general business conditions, than one that doesn't. But beyond that I don't know whether you could draw much of a conclusion. Mandel, presumably, is pretty much of an all cash company, and Barker might have rather substantial charge accounts in normal times because of the kind of business that it does.

QUESTION: In the case of Barker Brothers, the 1936-40 sales figures couldn't be used in comparison, could it, considering that in 1941-45 the company has expanded, I don't know how many times. Mandel, on the other hand, is still a one building company.

MR. GRAHAM: You may be right, though the actual figure on expansion of sales wouldn't quite bear that out. In 1945, which we have the full year for, the sales of Barker were $16.7 million, and those of Mandel were $27.5 million; and proportionatly Mandel sales expanded somewhat more from pre-war than Barker did, in spite of the fact that Barker opened up new stores, as you suggest, and Mandel didn't. I think you will find that the new stores, in many cases, are rather small matters as compared with the basic or original store which does the bulk of the business.

QUESTION: How did you arrive at your sales estimates for postwar years again? Thirty millions and twenty millions?

MR. GRAHAM: That was pretty much of a rough estimate, based upon the theory of an approximate doubling of the national income for post-war, as compared with pre-war. Rather than take the full 100% increase in the case of Barker and Mandel, it seemed advisable to cut that down somewhat, because during the war period, when national income had more than doubled, the sales of these two companies had not doubled. That would seem to be a reason for some caution. Twenty million and thirty million were convenient round amounts in that context.

We want to say just a word or two about the asset component in this method of evaluation, and then pass on to a completely different division of our subject.

We don't want to stress too much our ideas about assets in connection with valuation, because they are not customarily followed and we have no particular reason for believing that they are right. However, for your information, let me indicate how we feel about the asset situation.

We think that when the earning power value exceeds the asset value, some reduction should be made for that fact. And we have suggested that one-quarter of the difference be taken off--a very arbitrary figure. In other words, if Barker has a value of $17 in assets, and your earning power value is twenty-one, you would take off one-quarter of that difference of $4, and mark it down to 20. In many cases the difference is much greater, of course, and the adjustment is more important.

Where the assets exceed the earning power valuation, we do not value the company upward; because we are not very much impressed by assets that do not have earning power. There is, however, one rather important exception here, and that relates to working capital. Where the working capital exceeds the earning power value, we are impressed by experience to believe that there is some significance in that fact.

In summary fashion we are inclined to add half of the

difference to the earning power value, to allow for the excess
working capital which in some way or other tends to make itself
felt over the years. Sometimes you get it in a distribution; sometimes you get it in the sale of the property; sometimes you get it
because the company changes its policy and is able to use its
working capital more effectively than otherwise.

Where we valued Mandel at $30 a share--that is $9 million
dollars--of course there would be no mark-up for working capital,
because the working capital is only 5 million. But if your earning
value had been, say, the market price of 12-3/4, then you would
have added something to the fact that the working capital alone
is 5 million.

That is about all I want to say on the subject of asset
value, because, as I said before, I am not inclined to stress
that part of the technique of analysis.

I think this would be a good time to pause and take
stock a bit of what we have been trying to cover in this series
of lectures, before we go on to another division. You will recall
that we discussed, first, the market behavior in general of the
years 1941-45 in relation to economic changes that affected security
values. We considered new accounting factors that are involved in
the correct statement of the results that an individual company
may have achieved during the war and post-war periods. And we have
just recently finished our discussion of the technique of valuing
companies, based upon the capitalization of earning power and with
a minor adjustment for the asset picture.

Now I would like to return for a moment to the analyst's
view of Wall Street as a whole--that is, the scope of his own
activities in the securities markets and his approach to his
function of analyzing securities and drawing conclusions from his
analysis.

I suggest that there are two fundamentally different
approaches that the analyst may take to securities as a whole.

The first I call the conventional one, and that is based
primarily on quality and on prospects.

The second I call, in complimentary fashion, the
penetrating one, and that is based upon value.

Let us first attempt a brief description of these different approaches as they relate themselves to actual activities
of the analyst.

The conventional approach can be divided into three
separate ways of dealing with securities. The first is the
identification of "good stocks"--that is "strong stocks," "strong
companies," "well-entrenched companies", or "high quality companies.

Those companies presumably can be bought with safety at reasonable prices. That seems like a simple enough activity.

The second is the selection of companies which have better than average long-term prospects of growth in earnings. They are generally called "growth stocks."

The third is an intermediate activity, which involves the selection of companies which are expected to do better business in the near term than the average company. All three of those activities I call conventional.

The second approach divides itself into two sub-classes of action, namely, first, the purchase of securities generally whenever the market is at a low level, as the market level may be judged by analysts. The second is the purchase of special or individual securities at almost any time when their price appears to be well below the appraised or analyzed value.

Let me try to do a little appraising of the appraisers or the analysts themselves, and embark on a brief evaluation of these five lines of action which I have briefly described to you. Of course, I am expressing, basically, a personal opinion, which is derived from experience and observation and a great deal of thought; but it should not be taken as in any sense representing the standard view of the work of the security analyst.

The first division, you recall, was the simple identification of good companies and good stock; and one is inclined to be rather patronizing about a job as easy and elementary as that. My experience leads me to another conclusion. I think that it is the most useful of the three conventional approaches; provided only that a conscientious effort is made to be sure that the "good stock" is not selling above the range of conservative value.

Investors do not make mistakes, or bad mistakes, in buying good stocks at fair prices. They make their serious mistakes by buying poor stocks, particularly the ones that are pushed for various reasons. And sometimes--in fact, very frequently--they make mistakes by buying good stocks in the upper reaches of bull markets.

Therefore, the very simple kind of advice which keeps the investor in the paths of righteousness, or rather of rightness, I would say is very worthwhile advice--saying merely "These are good companies, and their prices are on the whole reasonable." I think also that that is the key to the policy of the well-established investment-counsel firms; and it accounts for their ability to survive, in spite of the fact that they are not in a very easy kind of business.

When you move from that simple and yet valuable occupation, namely, telling an investor that General Motors and General Electric

are safer things to buy than Barker Brothers at 25 3/4, for example-
when you move from that into the next activity, you are getting
into much more difficult ground, although it seems to be much more
interesting. And that is the selection of growth stocks, which
for a long while was the most popular or rather the best-regarded
type of activity by analysts.

        The successful purchase of growth stocks requires two
rather obvious conditions: first, that their prospects of growth
be realized; and, second, that the market has not already pretty
well discounted these growth prospects.

        These conditions do obtain with regard to some growth
stocks, as they are identified by analysts; and highly satisfactory
profits are made from that work. But the results vary a great
deal with the skill of the selector, and perhaps with "the luck
of the draw." It is quite questionable to my mind whether you can
establish a technique of a communicable sort--that a good instructor
can pass on to his pupil--by which you will be enabled to identify
those stocks not only which have good prospects of growth but
which have not already discounted pretty much those prospects in
the market.

        Let us put it in this way: I think at bottom success in
the identification of growth stocks comes from being smart or
shrewd, but I do not consider it a standard quality of good
security analysis to be smart or shrewd. Not that I have any
objection to that, but it just doesn't seem to me to fit into the
general pattern or canon of security analysis to require those
rather rare qualities.

        I might say rather that a security analyst should be
required to be wise, in the sense that he is technically competent,
that he is experienced, and that he is prudent. And I don't know
that wisdom of that sort is particularly well adapted to the
successful selection of growth stocks in a market that is so full
of surprises and disappointments in that field as in many others.
I have in mind many examples. If you take the chemical companies,
which have been the standard example of growth stocks for as long
back as I can remember, you will find that for a longperiod of
years their market behavior was quite unsatisfactory as compared
with other companies, merely because they had previously had a
great deal of popularity at a time when other companies were not
so popular.

        If you take the air transport stocks, the selection of
those securities for investment, based upon the idea of growth,
seems to me to have been an exceedingly speculative type of
thing; and I don't know how it could have been properly handled
under the techniques of well-established security analysis. As
you know, there are many, many hazards which exist in that kind
of industry, and in many others that have been regarded as having
unusual growth prospects.

Now let me pass on to the third activity of the conventional sort, which I think is done most constantly in day-by-day Wall Street organizations--the trade investigation, which leads one to believe that this industry or this company is going to have unusually good results in the next twelve months, and therefore the stock should be bought.

Permit me to say that I am most skeptical of this Wall Street activity, probably because it is the most popular form of passing the time of the security analyst. I regard it as naive in the extreme. The thought that the security analyst, by determining that a certain business is going to do well next year has thereby found something really useful, judged by any serious standards of utility, and that he can translate his discovery into an unconditional suggestion that the stock be bought, seems to me to be only a parody of true security analysis.

Take a typical case. What reason is there to think that because U. S. Plywood, for example, is going to do better in 1947 than it did in 1946, and National Department Stores will probably do worse in 1947 than it did in 1946--what reason is there to believe that U. S. Plywood should be purchased at 34 rather than National Department Stores at 17? There is scarcely any serious relationship between these concepts of next year's operations and the purchase and sale of the securities at the going market price; because the price of 34 for U. S. Plywood might have discounted very good earnings for three years, and the price of National Department Stores might theoretically have discounted poor earnings for three years. And in many cases that is not only theoretically so, but is actually so.

I would suggest, and this is a practical suggestion-- what I said before has been perhaps only a theoretical analysis in your eyes--that if you want to carry on the conventional lines of activity as analysts, that you impose some fairly obvious but nonetheless rigorous conditions on your own thinking, and perhaps on your own writing and recommending. In that way you can make sure that you are discharging your responsibilies as analysts. If you want to select good stocks--good, strong, respectable stocks-- for your clients, that's fine, I'm all for it. But determine and specify that the price is within the range of fair value when you make such a recommendation. And when you select growth stocks for yourself and your clients, determine and specify the round amount which the buyer at the current price is already paying for the growth factor, as compared with its reasonable price if the growth prospects were only average. And then determine and state whether, in the analyst's judgment, the growth prospects are such as to warrant the payment of the current price by a prudent investor.

I would like to see statements of that kind made in the security analyses and in circulars. It seems to me that you would then be getting some kind of defensible approach to this process of handing out recommendations.

And finally, in recommending a stock because of good near-term prospects, you should determine and state whether or not, in the analyst's judgment, the market price and its fairly recent market action has already reflected the expectations of the analyst. After you have determined that it hasn't, and that the thing has possibilities that have not been shown in the market action, then it would be at least a reasonable action on your part to recommend the stock because of its near-term prospects.

Have you any questions about this evaluation, perhaps somewhat biased, of the conventional activities of the security analyst?

QUESTION: Do you confine your near-term valuation, your Point 3, to just one year?

MR. GRAHAM: I am thinking more or less of between one and two years. Most people seem satisfied to talk about the next twelve months in this particular field.

Let us spend the next five minutes on the unconventional or penetrating type of security analysis, which emphasizes value.

The first division represents buying into the market as a whole at low levels; and that, of course, is a copybook procedure. Everybody knows that that is theoretically the right thing to do. It requires no explanation or defense; though there must be some catch to it, because so few people seem to do it continuously and successfully.

The first question you ask is, of course: "How do you know that the market price is low?" That can be answered pretty well, I think. The analyst identifies low market levels in relation to the past pattern of the market and by simple valuation methods such as those that we have been discussing. And bear in mind that the good analyst doesn't change his concept of what the earnings of the next five years are going to be just because the market happens to be pessimistic at one time, or optimistic at another. His views of average future earnings would change only because he is convinced that there has been some change of a very significant sort in the underlying factors.

Now he can also follow a mechanical system of operating in the market, if he wishes, like the Yale University method that many of you are familiar with. In this you sell a certain percentage of your stocks as they go up, or you convert a certain percentage of your bonds into stocks as they go down, from some median or average level.

I am sure that those policies are good policies, and they stand up in the light of experience. Of course, there is one very serious objection to them, and that is that "it is a long time between drinks" in many cases. You have to wait too long for

recurrent opportunities. You get tired and restless--especially
if you are an analyst on a payroll, for it is pretty hard to
justify drawing your salary just by waiting for recurrent low
markets to come around. And so obviously you want to do something
else besides that.

      The thing that you would naturally be led into, if you
are value-minded, would be the purchase of individual securities
that are undervalued at all stages of the security market. That
can be done successfully, and should be done--with one proviso,
which is that it is not wise to buy undervalued securities when the
general market seems very high. That is a particularly difficult
point to get across: for superficially it would seem that a high
market is just the time to buy the undervalued securities, because
their undervaluation seems most apparent then. If you could buy
Mandel at 13, let us say, with a working capital so much larger
when the general market is very high, it seems a better buy than
when the general market is average or low. Peculiarly enough,
experience shows that is not true. If the general market is very
high and is going to have a serious decline, then your purchase
of Mandel at 13 is not going to make you very happy or prosperous
for the time being. In all probability the stock will also
decline sharply in price in a break. Don't forget that if Mandel
or some similar company sells at less than your idea of value,
it sells so because it is not popular; and it is not going to get
more popular during periods when the market as a whole is declining
considerably. Its popularity tends to decrease along with the
popularity of stocks generally.

      QUESTION: Mr. Graham, isn't there what you might
call a negative kind of popularity, such as the variations of
Atchison? I mean, in a falling market, while it is perfectly true
that an undervalued security will go down, would it go down as fast
as some of the blue chips?

      MR. GRAHAM: In terms of percentage I would say
yes, on the whole. It will go down about as fast, because the
undervalued security tends to be a lower-priced security; and the
lower-priced securities tend to lose more percentagewise in any
important recessions than the higher ones. Thus you have several
technical reasons why it does not become really profitable to buy
undervalued securities at statistically high levels of the
securities market.

      If you are pretty sure that the market is too high, it
is a better policy to keep your money in cash or Government bonds
than it is to put it in bargain stocks. However, at other times--
and that is most of the time, of course--the field of undervalued
securities is profitable and suitable for analysts' activities.
We are going to talk about that at our next lecture.

Lecture No. 8   January 28, 1947.

CURRENT PROBLEMS IN SECURITY ANALYSIS

By
Benjamin Graham
****

MR. GRAHAM: At the last lecture we were talking about the work of the analyst of the unconventional kind who addresses himself to the field of undervalued securities. We had just about mentioned the fact that undervalued securities in the individual field offer opportunities practically at all times in the market, except when the general market itself is very high. We think that the investigation and the exploitation of undervalued securities, in what I would call normal markets, are the peculiar province of the security analyst.

You may very well ask some practical questions about that, such as: How, when, and why do undervalued securities establish their value in the market--and thus a profit to the purchaser? If they are unpopular at the time you buy them, why or how do these become popular?

The answer to that question is in part indefinite and empirical, based merely upon what we have seen occur through the years.

There does seem to be an inherent tendency in security markets for prices to move ultimately close to value. Consequently, if the value doesn't change while you are waiting for this to occur, you will not wait in vain for a profit--if we may accept average experience as a guide. That average experience shows, too, that the waiting period does not tend to be over-long. The price correction should happen, typically, within a two-year period, I would say. This makes possible a satisfactory average annual return from this type of operations.

The foregoing is a statement merely in regard to what tends to happen in the securities market in the field of undervalued securities. But beyond that we have the point that the correction of price-value disparities also arises at times from certain definite and specific developments in the company's affairs.

If, for example, the low price is due to the absence of dividends which are earned and should be paid, the company may remedy this deficiency and then the price will rise. That, of course, is the simplest type of development.

You may take as a current and concrete example the situation in Cities Service Preferred stock on the one hand, as

compared with Alleghany Prior Preferred on the other. In both
cases dividends have been permitted to accumulate over a long
period of years, although each company's operations would have
permitted the full payment of the dividend.

In the case of Cities Service, the company finally has
taken steps to take care of the accumulated dividends--and in fact
to pay off the principal of the stock as well--and you have recently
had a market response to this move.

What has happened here has not been that the intrinsic
value of Cities Service Preferred has increased by reason of
developments affecting earning power or asset value; but the price
has risen because finally the company is making a belated effort
to take care of its obligations to the Preferred holders.

On the other hand, the Alleghany Prior Preferred, which
is very much the same situation, is not benefitting from any such
provision, and thus you have a difference in the market action.
At the end of 1945 Cities Service Preferred sold at 145; and now
in a generally lower market it is selling at 157, because it has
a plan to pay off the Preferred dividends. At the end of 1945
Alleghany Prior Preferred sold at 70½ and is now selling at 58,
because it has no plan to pay off its Prior Preferred dividends.

Thus you see that the price--which, of course, as practical
analysts you are very much interested in--does depend largely in
a number of cases, such as these--upon what action the company
itself will take.

It follows that, in dealing with undervalued securities,
the analyst is likely to become greatly interested in specific
corporate developments, and therefore in proper corporate policies.
And from being interested in corporate policies, he may pass over
into being critical of wrong policies and actively agitating to
bring about correct policies--all of which he considers to be in
the stockholders' interests. For it is true that in a fairly
large percentage of cases the undervaluation in the market can be
removed by proper action by or in the corporation.

Consequently, by insensible stages of reasoning, the
specialist in undervalued securities finds himself turning into
that abomination of Wall Street known as a disgruntled stockholder.

I want to say a word about disgruntled stockholders.
The trouble with stockholders, in my humble opinion, is that not
enough of them are disgruntled. And one of the great troubles with
Wall Street is that it cannot distinguish between a mere trouble-
maker or "strike-suiter" in corporation affairs and a stockholder
with a legitimate complaint which deserves attention from his
management and from his fellow stockholders.

Tonight, and probably in the next lecture, I would like
to spend quite a little time in developing in a concrete way the
relationship between (a) undervalued securities, which is our
general subject; (b) defective corporate policies, which in many
cases create undervalued securities; and (c) the correct stockholders' attitude, which could improve the corporation policy and
improve the market price of the securities--but which is very
rarely done because the stockholders just don't have enough common
sense to do it.

I would like to take as a case history for this purpose
not a single company, as one ordinarily does, but an entire industry
and that is the fire and casualty insurance industry.

There are always two ways of looking at investment
problems: one is the superficial way and the other is the
penetrating way. I think the more you penetrate into the insurance
industry, the more unusual and surprising things you find out about
the character of that business in relation to the stockholders'
viewpoint and the stockholders' position.

You might call this a very wonderful industry, "where
every prospect pleases and only the stockholder is vile." That,
of course, was not always true. Our case history illustrates a
fundamental element in corporate and security developments, which
is this: On almost every case the position of the stockholder was
a satisfactory one at the early stages, and he had no reason to be
particularly critical of corporate policies. The impairment of
his situation by developments that are contrary to his interest
generally comes about in a slow and gradual way, which he does not
realize and which his advisers and the experts in the field fail
to realize as well.

If you take the insurance business, for example, you
might go to the headquarters of analysis and advice on the subject,
which is "Best's Digest of Insurance Stocks.." If you refer to the
first issue of this Digest, in 1931, you will read a paragraph
somewhat as follows:

"The reasons for the increased popularity of insurance
stocks among investors generally are many. The stock
of well-managed insurance companies is an excellent long term
investment, affording unusual security, substantial and
increasing return, and reasonable assurance of enhancement
in value. Insurance is an indispensable factor in modern
economic life--an investment factor of prime importance.
The volume of insurance transactions necessarily increases
not only in proportion to the growth of the entire nation,
but actually at a greater rate, because the increasing
complexities of modern industry constantly give rise to
the need for entirely new forms of insurance, and also
because the public is constantly becoming better educated
to the necessities for carrying adequate amounts of insurance
of many different types."

That describes the situation in insurance stocks that
existed during most of the 1920's. Of course, the first Digest
was published in 1931, and a lot of trouble had already started,
but it was a bit retroactive and wistful in this description of
the industry.

We shall find the situation in the 1920's illustrated
by some examples that I selected and have put on the blackboard.

COMPARATIVE STOCKHOLDERS EQUITY AND MARKET PRICE OF THREE INSURANCE STOCKS.

	1927 Equity 12/31	1927 High Bid in Year	1945 Equity 12/31	1945 High Bid in Year	1946 Equity 12/31	1946 Bid 12/31
Amer. Equitable Insurance Actual	47	95	47	26	est. 39	16
(Adjusted *)	(70)	(141)				
New Amsterdam Casualty Actual	41	80	48	36½	48	26
(Adjusted *)	(26½)	(52)				
North River Insurance Actual	67	100	31¼	26½	est. 30	21
(Adjusted *)	(20-3/4)	(31)				

*Adjusted to compare with 1945 and 1946 figures.

I have taken three companies, each of which illustrates
a whole group of shares. In alphabetical order they are American
Equitable Insurance, a fire company; New Amsterdam Casualty, a
casualty company; and North River Insurance, a fire company. (The
figures appear in the table.)

At the end of 1927 American Equitable had an equity,
as ordinarily figured, of $47 for the stockholder. Its 1927
high price was 95, about the end of the year.

New Amsterdam Casualty had an equity of 41, and its
high price was 80.

North River Insurance had an equity of 20 3/4, adjusted
in this case to present capitalization, and its high price, also
adjusted, was 31.

A very satisfactory situation from the standpoint of
stockholders is here reflected in the market's reaction, because
in a general way the market was paying between 50 and 100 per cent

more than the equity or book value for shares. This was in a
market which was roughly similar to the market of 1945, the
Dow-Jones average selling as high as 202 in that year and 196
in 1945.

But when we go over into 1945 we find a very different
situation. American Equitable still has an equity of 47 for its
then stock--not the same as the 1927 stock--but its highest price
was only 26.

New Amsterdam had an equity of 48, but its highest bid
price was 36½.

North River Insurance had an equity of 31¼, and its
high bid was 26½.

Nearly all the insurance companies were selling in 1945
at substantial discounts from their liquidation values or equities,
as customarily figured. This condition existed under very
favorable general market conditions.

Best and Company issued the 16th annual edition of the
"Digest of Insurance Stocks" in 1946, and again discusses the
insurance stocks as investments. Surprisingly enough it uses the
identical words as it did in 1931--with one change, which I think
is a little amusing. In 1931 it said, "There are many reasons for
the increasing popularity of insurance stocks," but in 1946 it
says, "There are many reasons for the lasting popularity of
insurance stocks among investors." (Words underlined by Mr. Graham)

The rest of the discussion is in the identical words of
1931. This point illustrates the fact that a lot of things may
happen over a period of sixteen or twenty years and not be noticed
at all by people whose business it really is to notice them.

What has happened to the insurance business between 1927,
let us say, and 1945? If this were 1927 and I were lecturing on
insurance stocks, I certainly wouldn't talk about it in terms of a
disgruntled stockholder. Discussing it now, I am going to talk
about it in terms of a disgruntled stockholder. The reason is that
conditions have changed very considerably from the stockholders'
standpoint--although not very much from the standpoint of anybody
else interested, namely the management, the agents, or the
policyholders of the insurance companies. They have all fared quite
well in the intervening period.

Let us develop the change in the situation by means of
the North River Insurance Company. North River was selected
as an example of a high-grade, well thought of company, which has
had about average results. It is not average in one respect and
that is in age. The North River Insurance Company was established
quite a long while ago, in 1822, and it has paid dividends
continuously since 1838--for a period of 108 years.

It had originally $350,000 of capital, and now its total
funds for stockholders are about 25 million dollars, or 70 times
the original amount. You would assume, I think, that the North
River Insurance Company would represent not only a well-established
company--which indeed it is--but a very attractive company to
have money invested in. It is not an attractive company to have
money invested in today, and we can show arithmetically or
mathematically why it isn't. That I think is the most interesting
part of this discussion.

The North River Company in 1927 had an underwriting
profit of $1.02 a share, investment income of $1.37--presumably
after taxes in both cases, since it showed a balance of $2.39
for the stock, which was around $11\frac{1}{2}$ per cent on the invested
capital or equity. That, of course, is by no means an unsatisfactory
showing for a high grade company, and it would account for and
probably justify the stock's selling at a premium of approximately
50 per cent above its equity.

In 1945 the underwriting profit was less than half; the
investment income was down somewhat; the earnings were subject to
a large tax. Consequently the balance was $1.26 per share, which
was not more than half of the earnings of 1927, although the
equity had gone up fifty per cent in the meantime. We find that
the stock earned approximately four per cent on its investment
in 1945--and by investment I mean the stockholders' investment, not
the total investments owned by the company, which were larger--
as against about three times as much in 1927.

Thus, in comparing pretty representative years, in the
respective periods, we find that the stockholders seem to have lost
two-thirds of their former earning power.

We should make some reference to underwriting conditions
in the two years that we are comparing. Those of you who are
familiar with the fire insurance business know that the situation
in underwriting has been unsatisfactory in the last three years,
because losses have been very large and rates have not been
remunerative on the whole. However, there have been some companies
that have done pretty well on their underwriting, even in 1945.
The North River Company was one of them and earned about four
per cent on its underwriting business in 1945, which is more or
less its average earning power for the past ten years. Consequently
no adjustment need be made for 1945 results in this case on the
ground that general business in insurance was very bad.

If you analyze this picture in further detail you will
find that several things have happened to cut the earning power
down from about twelve per cent to only four per cent. These
are summarized in the table on the board.

T A B L E

NORTH RIVER INSURANCE CO.

(Per share, adjusted to 12/31/45 capitalization)

	1927	1945
Price Dec. 31	31	24
Liquidating Value	$20.7	$31.2
(Price Dow-Jones Ind. Ave.)	(202)	(193)
Earned from Underwriting	$1.02	$ .46
Investment Income	1.37	1.16
Less Federal Tax	--	- .36
Operating Earnings	2.39	1.26
Per Dollar of Liquidating Value:		
Premiums	.82	.36
Underwriting Profit	.05	.015
Invested Assets	1.45	1.18
Investment Income before Tax	.066	.037
Total Income before Tax	.116	.052
Federal Tax	--	.012
Net Operating Earnings	.116	.04
% of Underwriting Profit to Premiums	6%	4%*
% of Investment Income to Assets	4.6%	3.1%*

*Before Taxes

- -

In the first place, the amount of premiums per dollar of equity has been cut in half. Secondly, the underwriting margin on those premiums is down from six per cent to four per cent. That combination gives you less than half the former underwriting profit per dollar of investment.

The invested assets per dollar of stockholders' equity have been reduced from $1.45 to $1.18; and the rate of return is down from 4½ per cent--apparently after taxes--to 3.1 per cent before taxes. There has thus been a reduction in every one of the four categories which contribute to earning power--namely the amount of earning assets and earning business per dollar, and the rate of profit on those two per dollar. The result is, as I have said, that the over-all figures have come down tremendously.

Now when we look at North River not comparatively but absolutely, we reach the conclusion, and it is a very strange one, that the nature of the business as it is now set up does not permit the company to earn a decent return on the stockholders' equity. The trouble with North River is not that business is bad, nor that the management is incompetent, but that the nature of the fire insurance industry as it has developed and as it is being generally carried on will not permit the stockholders to get a fair return.

Let us analyze that statement. What would we mean by a fair return to the stockholders? I am suggesting, subject to disagreement, that you would expect a business of this kind to earn six per cent, on the average, on the value of the stockholders' equity and pay out four per cent, retaining the other two per cent for expansion.

In the earlier years it was quite possible for the fire insurance companies to do that. Today, as you can see from this North River example, it is quite impossible.

The underwriting business itself has turned out to be an extraordinarily unimportant thing one way or the other from the standpoint of the owners. It is certainly very important from the standpoint of the companies, but when you look at it from the standpoint of the stockholders, it is very hard not only to get excited about it but even seriously interested in it.

Let me give you the reason in a rather impressive way. The insurance business seems to be divided--I am speaking now of fire insurance exclusively--into three kinds of companies: the unprofitable ones, the more or less average ones, and a few really profitable companies. The best of the lot, from the standpoint of profit, is the St. Paul Fire and Marin e Insurance Company, which shows an average profit for the past ten years of ten per cent on its business. That is very much higher than the average of the industry, which might be on the order of three or four per cent on the business. St. Paul Fire and Marine, which is three times as profitable as the average company, can earn all of 4% for its stockholders on their investment out of the insurance business, on the basis of earning ten per cent on its 1946 premiums. In other words, it can earn $2.80 a share, after allowing for a 38 per cent corporation tax on these profits, on a net asset value of $72, and that is less than four per cent. Here we have the maximum earnings that it is possible to get out of the insurance business from an extraordinarily successful company.

On the other hand, if we take the least successful of a long list of companies, the American Reserve Insurance Company, which managed to lose an average of 4% for the last ten years on its business, we find, after crediting it with a tax saving through the loss, that it is losing about two per cent per year on its capital through the insurance business. And if we take North River as an average company--it is a little bit better than the average--we find this extraordinary thing: that if they earn four per cent on 9 million dollars of premiums, which was the 1945 figure, and after they pay income tax on it, they have left 28¢ a share--which is less than one per cent on the book value of the stock.

From these varied examples we conclude that from the standpoint of the stockholders all the operations of the fire insurance business--which are the basis of such great encomiums in the analyses and at all the insurance company conventions-- have been of negligible importance, whether they are profitable or whether they are mildly unprofitable.

When we come to the question of the other part of the earnings, which arises from investments, we find again that it is not in the cards to earn any substantial amounts on the stockholders' equity. If we take North River insurance as an example, we see that they are able to earn $1.16 a share before taxes, and the tax portion thereof is probably on the order of 30¢, or thereabouts; so that they are not able to earn from investments more than three per cent after taxes for their stock.

The combination, therefore, in the case of North River Insurance is roughly a one per cent earning power from their insurance business, and a three per cent earning power from their investment business. That combination just doesn't pay out for the stockholders. It doesn't justify the investment of money in that sort of business.

That is my analysis of the present status of an average insurance company.

I am sure that there will be someone here who will want to raise some questions about that, before I go on to "another part of the forest."

QUESTION: In connection with investment income, isn't it possible that the method in which that is determined might be conservative? In other words, investment income, as I understand it, would probably be income from interest, dividends, and excluding capital appreciation.

MR. GRAHAM: Yes. I am glad you raised the question, because I omitted any reference to the question of capital appreciation or depreciation in insurance company investments.

Speaking about that, I would like to go back to the reasons for the popularity of insurance company shares in the 1920's. The analyses that used to be made at that time indicated that the insurance stockholder was a very fortunate person, because he had three different and valuable sources of income. One was the insurance business, which was supposed to be a very good industry, although there was no analysis of how much it contributed in earnings in those days. It was taken for granted that it was a good business for the stockholder.

Then it was said that you got the interest on money, not only your own money, but you got interest and dividends also on a lot of money that the policyholders had left with you in the form of unearned premiums and unpaid losses, and so on. Thus, for every dollar of your own, you had a total of about two dollars working for you, drawing investment income.

The third advantage was that you had extremely capable investment managements putting your money in securities and making a lot of profits for you.

Of course they made profits for you in the 1920's when the market was going up, and of course they lost a great deal of money in the early 1930's when the market was going down. The same thing happened in 1937-38, when they made a lot of money up to March '37, then they lost a great deal in the ensuing decline.

The net of all this history, I am pretty sure, is that today's sophisticated investors are not willing to pay very much for the ability of insurance managements to make capital gains for them over the years. It turns out that we do not have the type of check-ups and careful analysis of insurance company investment results that we have in the case of investment trusts, because the business does not lend itself so easily to that kind of thing. But it can be done. I am going to give you some figures on American Equitable Insurance Company over a twenty-year period, to indicate how that company made out for that period of time with its investments as well as with its underwritings.

But on the whole, just answering the specific question asked, no investor today--and I don't think any analyst--is willing to give the insurance business any special credit for ability to make profits on the principal value of its securities. It will make profits in good years and it will lose money in bad years from that department. That may be doing it an injustice; but that I am sure is the general opinion of security analysts at the present time.

Are there other questions about that?

QUESTION: Would you care to take a minute to differentiate between premiums and underwriting profit? That is a little technical. What is underwriting profit?

MR. GRAHAM: Underwriting profit is the profit earned from the insurance business as such. It consists of the balance left after you pay the losses and the expenses of the underwriting business. It includes, moreover, a certain component known as the increase in the unearned premium reserve, which is a technicality. It is generally accepted that the liabilities shown on the balance sheet for "unearned premium reserves" include, to the extent of forty per cent ordinarily, an amount that is really the stockholders' equity. When that figure goes up, the insurance profits for the year are increased accordingly, and conversely. Thus you really have two parts to your underwriting results: one, the straight result, and the other the equity in the increase or decrease in the unearned premium reserve.

I do want to say something about the method of calculating liquidating values, or equities, in this business, but I will delay that for a while.

QUESTION: What of the possibilities of increasing the underwriting profits, rather of raising rates in underwriting business? You always get a lull after a war, when the insurance on property has to be marked up after the replacement value advances.

MR. GRAHAM: In answering that question now, I would like to distinguish very sharply between recent results and long-term average results. The recent results of the fire business have been bad. Most companies, I think, showed losses for 1946--the figures are not out yet--and about half of them, perhaps, showed losses for 1945.

The results that I have been dealing with have been ten-year average figures, and I think that they pretty fairly represent what you can expect over the years in the insurance business. It may be that the results will be a little better in the next ten years than they were in the last ten years, but I don't believe that an insurance analyst or an investor ought to count particularly upon that. He should count upon their being better in the next five years than they were in the last two or three, which is of course a different matter.

QUESTION: Why do companies like the American Reserve or even the North River stay in business, then?

MR. GRAHAM: The North River Company stays in business, of course, because it has been in existence for 126 years, and has built up a large business, which has increased over the years, which has been satisfactory to the people running the business, to its agents, and to its policyholders. Whether it is now satisfactory to the stockholders I don't think has ever been asked, and I don't think such questions are asked in any of these companies.

I have read a number of reports of fire insurance companies to their stockholders. They consist generally of a one-page balance sheet and a few pages listing the securities owned. The question of how profitable is the business, is just not discussed. I suppose it would be ungentlemanly to raise the point.

QUESTION: Do your figures here show underwriting profit as reported, or is some adjustment made such as the Best adjustments for unearned premiums?

MR. GRAHAM: These include the unearned premium adjustment, which is pretty standard. In fact, the companies themselves, in many cases, indicate what that amounts to in their discussions at their annual meetings. It is really standard procedure.

In the casualty business there is still another adjustment, which I will mention later on--the difference between one kind of reserve and another kind of reserve method.

QUESTION: Well, one of the reasons for stockholders not knowing anything about insurance companies is the fact that, I think, until recently they didn't publish any profit or loss statements. They just gave balance sheets on the statement, just like the bank did.

MR. GRAHAM: Yes. If I were a stockholder in an insurance company, I would like to know whether the business was profitable enough, and I would ask. But apparently the stockholders in the insurance companies don't ask that question, to the extent of requiring that the figures be analyzed or presented in the annual reports.

The casualty companies, interestingly enough, tend to publish rather elaborate reports, with a good deal of information. One reason, perhaps, is that the casualty business has been quite profitable in the last ten years.

QUESTION: Don't you think the stockholders' complacency is caused by the fact that the early investor in insurance companies--such as Continental, or what is called the "Home Group."--has done very well over the last twenty years with his money. Whether he has been lulled to sleep is another thing, but I think that has been the cause of it.

MR. GRAHAM: I am not in a position to tell you what happened in the last twenty years to every one of these companies. But I do know that in the fire group some companies have done very badly for twenty years; and a company like North River, which I believe is pretty representative, has started off doing very well and is finishing up in a situation which does not permit it to do really well for its stockholders. I don't believe that this analysis would be subject to much change if you took other companies. You might find one or two exceptions, such as the St. Paul Fire and Marine. But they are extraordinarily few.

QUESTION: Is the competition of Mutuals a factor here?

MR. GRAHAM: I don't know whether that really is a factor. It might be. But the insurance companies endeavor to obtain higher rates when they need them by application to the various insurance boards, and there is always a lag in getting them.

QUESTION: The solicitors for the mutuals insistently cite expenses cheaper than the stock company. That is one of their big points. That is to say, in the form of commissions to agents. Net costs to the policy holder.

MR. GRAHAM: I shouldn't be surprised if that were so. There is reason to believe that the scale of commissions paid on fire insurance policies has been too high--the commissions paid to agents. It doesn't take a great deal of salesmanship in my opinion to sell a fire insurance policy. It does take quite a bit perhaps to sell a life insurance policy. The fire commissions have been pretty large, and I think that in some cases recently the state insurance departments have hesitated to permit premiums raises on the ground that the commissions to agents have been too high. At least so I am informed, but I will not state that as a fact.

QUESTION: The casualty men always stress cost to the policyholders.

MR. GRAHAM: In the mutuals, too? Well, in the casualty field, in spite of the competition with the mutual companies, the stock companies have been able to earn a very considerable sum of money for their stockholders.

Are there other questions about that?

QUESTION: To get back to a point that might be elementary. I am not at all familiar with these industries. You have 1927 and 1945 statistics on the board. I can see why there has been a decline in investment income; but even if it is repetitious, will you explain why there has been that sharp decline in underwriting profit, and whether that is a transitory situation or will it continue?

MR. GRAHAM: The decline in the underwriting profit of North River is due to two factors: one is the profit per dollar of insurance written, which went down from about six per cent to four per cent for those two years. It is difficult to say whether that is a permanent thing or not. I am inclined to think that there is a slight tendency for that rate to go down through the years.

The more important fact is that the amount of premiums written by this company, per dollar of stockholders' equity, has been cut in two. Therefore, with the same rate of profit you would only earn half as much on your stock.

That is just like saying you now have only fifty cents of sales per dollar of capital, instead of a dollar of sales.

The reason for that is very interesting, and I would like to comment on it a bit. What has happened is that these companies have built up their stockholders' equity in various ways in the period to a much greater extent than they built up their premiums. The result is that from the standpoint of good results for the stockholders, they seem to have much too much capital per dollar of business done in 1945.

Of course, the insurance companies will insist that is not true. They will say that the more capital they have the better the policyholders are, and therefore the better the stockholders are. They will also say that they expect to do very much more business in the future, and therefore they should have the capital available for the expanding business. But the fact remains that in dollars and cents you have the situation that the North River Company had 25 million dollars of stockholders' capital and did about 9 million dollars of business in 1945, which is a very small amount of business per dollar of capital. In 1927 they did a somewhat larger amount of business with less than half the amount of capital.

No attention has been paid to that matter by anyone, that is by any stockholder. As far as the management is concerned, the more capital they have, the better off they are. There isn't the slightest doubt about that.

QUESTION: Haven't they got more money to invest in stocks?

MR. GRAHAM: They have more money to invest in stocks, but that is no special advantage to the stockholder because he has more money of his own invested. The question is what about the rate of return, and that has gone down too, of course.

There is a better answer to your question. Because they have more capital, the amount of investment per dollar of capital goes down. The reason is that in addition to investing the stockholders' capital they invest other moneys that come out of the conduct of the business. The more capital there is in relation to the business, the less proportionate excess do they have. That is shown in this figure: In 1927 they had $1.45 of invested assets per dollar of stockholder's capital, and now they have only $1.18. So they lost out in that respect too.

Now, I might suggest that somebody should raise the question, "What can the stockholders do to get a decent return on their investment on the North River Insurance Company?" Let us assume it was a matter for the stockholders to decide, which would be a very extraordinary suggestion for anyone to make--elementary as it sounds in theory. Here is a possible answer: Suppose you re-established the relationship between capital and premiums that

existed in 1927, when things were quite satisfactory, by simply
returning to the stockholders the excess capital in relation to
the business done. If you did that, you would be able to get
the earnings of about six per cent on your capital and to pay the
four per cent dividend on your capital, which I suggested might be
a definition of a reasonable return to the stockholder. That could
happen because, when you take out fifteen dollars a share from the
present thirty-one dollars--and you have left only sixteen
dollars to earn money on for the stockholder--you are reducing
your earnings only by the net investment income on the $15 with-
drawn, which is on the order of, say, 40¢ at the most. Thus you
would earn about 85¢ on the remaining investment of $16 and you
would get reasonably close to the six per cent which you need.

        That is a method that will not recommend itself to
insurance company managements, but which at least has some
arithmetical validity as far as the stockholders are concerned.

        Are there any other questions about this analysis with
regard to the North River Company?

        QUESTION: I don't quite understand. What is the
reason for the decline in the volume, dollar volume, of premiums
underwritten? Is it a question of growth and competition in the
industry? Would you not expect the over-all dollar amount of
premiums to increase over a period of twenty-odd years?

        MR. GRAHAM: The situation is this: For the country
as a whole net premiums written by fire companies grew in volume
from $966 million in 1927 to $1,226 million in 1945. That would
represent an increase of about one-third.

        The North River Company had $9.1 million in premiums in
1945, and $10.9 million in 1927. That was a reduction of about
16 per cent. It is pretty clear that the North River Company
individually went back in that period of time. Many of the other
companies, which increased their premiums, however, increased them
by absorbing other companies over the twenty-year period. Also a
good deal of the insurance written was taken by new fire subsidiaries
of casualty companies, and so on. It may well be that the typical
company which didn't go through corporate changes, but just stuck
to its old setup, might have had a situation not so different from
the North River Company, namely, a decline in premiums.

        It is important to point out that the rate of premiums
per thousand dollars of insurance went down very much from 1927
to 1945. The companies gave more to the policyholder for their
money. The result is that their premium income suffered, and does
not reflect the true growth in the amount of coverage extended.

        QUESTION: Did North River sell additional shares during
that eighteen-year period?

MR. GRAHAM: Yes. I made an error in my previous statement that I want to correct. I said that the North River company had retained its old position. That was not right. They took over another company, which represents about one-fifth of their total capitalization. That means they added about twenty-five per cent, presumably, to their business by absorbing another company in that period of time, so they should have shown an increase in their business. Exactly why this company didn't do it, I don't know.

QUESTION: Isn't the North River one of a group of companies?

MR. GRAHAM: Yes, it is operated by the Crum and Forster organization.

QUESTION: They may have stuck the premiums in some of their other companies.

MR. GRAHAM: That might be the reason. That is another interesting question that arises in the treatment of stockholders' interest by insurance company managements. Many of the insurance companies are part of so-called "fleets" or groups of companies, and you find some very surprising things in those fleets. Some of the companies tend to be quite profitable, and others in the same group tend to be unprofitable. When you ask for an explanation, as I have done in one case, you may be a bit surprised at the kind of explanation you get. The thing that surprises me always is that the insurance people never talk in terms of what happens to the stockholder. They always talk in terms of what happens to the business as such. You can find many business reasons why Company A should be profitable and Company B should be unprofitiable--but no reason that will satisfy the stockholder of Company B, in that case.

Any other questions about that?

If we now go over to the other two companies, we will find what seems to be a simpler kind of situation. For the issue involved is not what would seem to be the inherent unprofitability of a business that was previously profitable enough--i.e., a new unprofitability growing out of very gradual developments--but quite a different state of affairs.

I shall outline the problems of the other two companies to you in the next five minutes. In the following lecture I want to go into detail, because in some respects I think the matter is fascinating.

The American Equitable Insurance Company transacts what must be called an unprofitable business--because in the past twenty years they succeeded in losing two million dollars in the aggregate out of their insurance operations, and in more than half

the years they lost money. Our problem there is to deal with the
question which has been raised on the floor already: Why should
the stockholders permit the continuance of a business which seems
to be by all definitions of success an unsuccessful one, and a
business which the stockholders could very readily dispose of or
turn out of?

It is a characteristic of the insurance business that
the assets are, on the whole, very liquid and the liabilities can
be disposed of without too much trouble. They can be transferred
to other companies. There is no problem of any real significance
in winding up an unsuccessful insurance company business in the
fire or casualty field. At bottom, it is a question of the net
price realized.

The New Amsterdam Casualty Company is much more interesting than American Equitable. The New Amsterdam Casualty Company
has been extremely profitable over the past 10 years. It has a
very fine record, but the stockholders are not allowed to participate in its success by the simple expedient of keeping the dividend
down to a figure which can't possibly carry the asset value of the
shares. The New Amsterdam Casualty Company has built up an asset
value of about fifty dollars a share. It has insisted upon paying
a one-dollar dividend since 1943, although in this time average
earnings have been on the order of four dollars or more. The
result is that the market has decided that one dollar in dividends
is not worth more than thirty-six dollars and a half at the top,
and at the end of 1946 it was not worth more than twenty-six
dollars. That is the situation which has existed for years past,
and for all we know might exist for years to come.

It is a relatively simple matter to state the problems
involved for the stockholder or the analyst of these two companies--
and simple also to formulate the solutions. But whether there is
any practical value in that analysis and those solutions it is
extremely difficult to tell. I think that much more depends upon
your own response to this analysis than you think. If you, as a
group of representative security analysts, will follow this
presentation and reasoning and agree that they are sound, and agree
that something should be done, and are willing to do something about
these situations--then you can not only aid stockholders generally
to obtain fair and reasonable treatment, but you can also benefit
yourselves as purchasers of undervalued securities. For undervalued
security situations to a very great extent are action situations.
Where, as very often happens, the action takes place by itself you
don't have to do anything. But in other cases it may be up to
you to take the action in order to remove the undervaluation. Thus
you may make certain that a profit is realized within a reasonably
short time, instead, possibly, of a very long time or never.

Lecture No. 9   February 11, 1947

CURRENT PROBLEMS IN SECURITY ANALYSIS

By
Benjamin Graham
****

MR. GRAHAM: In this lecture it is my purpose to
continue our analysis of insurance stocks, particularly the
American Equitable and New Amsterdam examples referred to two
weeks ago.

As a preliminary, it might be well to devote a little
time to discussing some aspects of security analysis technique
relating to the calculation of the asset values and earnings of
insurance companies. This should be part of your professional
knowledge as analysts.

On the blackboard two weeks ago we set forth asset
values and market prices for three insurance companies both in 1927
and 1945. In the case of North River, the 1927 figures were
adjusted to the 1945 capitalization, so that the data for both
years are comparable. In the case of American Equitable and New
Amsterdam, we used the actual figures in 1927, since which time
many capital changes have taken place in both companies.

Between 1926 and 1945 American Equitable participated in
four mergers, made one large offering of stock to its stockholders,
paid back some cash in connection with one merger, paid two large
stock dividends or split-ups, and then reversed the process by
two "split-downs".

Now, all those operations can be summarized as follows:
If at the end of 1927 you owned one share with a then book value
of 47, you would have paid in $20 more and received $7.20 in cash
adjustment, and thus your investment would be $59.80; and for that
you now have four-fifths of a share. Since American Equitable
still has a book value of $47 a share, the four-fifths that you
have would be worth $38, as compared with $59.80 that you would
have paid in throughout the period. Although it appears in the
table as if you are in the same position now as you were twenty
years ago, in regard to equity, actually you have lost about one-
third of your initial equity in that company in the twenty years.

In the New Amsterdam case the result is quite different.
There if you had an investment worth in 1927, 41 at book value,
you would have paid in for rights about $8 a share, bringing your
investment up to forty-nine dollars; and you would have obtained,
through the rights and a split-up, 1.85 shares of stock. Hence,

at the present $48 book value per share, the share you owned would now have a book value of $89, as compared with $49 paid in--an increase of eighty per cent in value over the twenty years.

Hence you can see that, while on the board the book value results seem approximately the same for the two companies over the twenty years, actually when you allow for adjustments you find American Equitable stockholders suffered a considerable shrinkage and the New Amsterdam stockholders had a considerable gain.

Is there any question about that particular statement of fact as to the two companies?

Going on to the more general question as to how these equities are computed, it is necessary to point out a number of special factors which exist in insurance companies which differ from book value factors in other enterprises. In the standard type of corporate balance sheet, you figure book value by taking capital stock plus surplus plus such reserves as are voluntary and not regarded as equivalent to liabilities; and you deduct intangible assets, if any.

In the insurance companies you have several other factors to consider. For one thing, you must consider the difference between consolidated figures and those of the parent company only. In most corporations a consolidated report appears as a matter of course. That is not true in the insurance company business. Many companies publish only their parent company's balance sheet in the first instance, and you have to look around for the consolidated figures, where they own subsidiaries.

The next point is that part of the unearned premium reserve, which is considered by the insurance departments as a full liability, is generally accepted by all authorities as a portion of the stockholders' equity.

In the fire-insurance companies it is standard practice to regard forty per cent of the unearned premium reserve as belonging to the stockholders. That practice may be considered in the nature of prepaid expense, if you wish to use that accounting term.

In the casualty business the percentage varies from thirty to forty per cent, depending partly on who is doing the computing and partly on the company that is being considered.

You have also the difference between bonds shown on an amortized basis, which is standard practice in the published balance sheet, and bonds taken at the market price, which appears as a footnote in many corporate reports.

You have also the factor of unadmitted assets, which include claims against unauthorized companies. Where an insurance company has reinsurance with a concern--let us say particularly Lloyds of London--which is not authorized to do business in the states in which this insurance company operates--it cannot show as an asset for purposes of determining its financial strength its claim against such unauthorized company. This claim may be perfectly good from the stockholders' standpoint, but it does not appear in the calculation made on the reports to the state authorities.

QUESTION: What is the reason for that; do you know?

MR. GRAHAM: Well, the reason is simple enough. The state authorities say that only companies which are subject to regulation by these authorities can be recognized as good debtors of any given insurance company--the theory being that perhaps the claim is of no value at all, since the state authority does not have jurisdiction over the unauthorized company. There is a basic reason why Lloyds is not authorized to do business in American states, but that I will not go into.

Then you have another matter which should be mentioned. It is not particularly important now, but it was at one time. There are different methods of calculating liabilities for future payments. One is called the statutory method and the case method. Under the former a certain percentage of premiums, in some cases sixty per cent in other cases sixty-five per cent, has to be assumed as the amount of losses that will be taken. In the case method, the company calculates what its losses will be, based on its own experience. That relates to various types of casualty insurance, not to fire insurance.

All those adjustments that I mentioned show up in the calculation of the liquidating value of insurance companies. I have here two examples which illustrate concretely the effect of some of these adjustments, perhaps all of them.

Let us take, first, the American Automobile Insurance Company. You start with the capital stock and surplus shown in the "convention report"--$35.80 per share. That includes marking up their bonds to the market price from their amortized value To that is added the equity in the unearned premium reserve at thirty per cent, which is the percentage allowed by Standard Statistics in their calculations. That gives you the stockholders' equity of $41.75 per share, as you will see it in the Standard Statistics analysis.

If we go on to Best and Company's analysis--and Best and Company is one of the recognized authorities, perhaps the recognized authority in the analysis of insurance stocks--you find first they add one dollar to unearned premium reserve equity, because they

accept thirty-five per cent as applicable; and secondly they add
as much as $5.75 here to write down the liabilities from the
statutory basis to the case basis. That gives them $48.50 as their
equity per share, as shown in "Best's Digest" for 1946.

However, in a footnote they tell you that if the additional
equity in subsidiaries is counted, you will get a final stockholders' equity of $60.30. That is the figure given by the
elaborate analysis made by Geyer and Company, one of the dealers
in insurance stocks.

The difference between the Standard Statistics figure
of 41.75 and the Geyer figure of 60.30 is a very substantial one
indeed. It means that if you are interested in liquidating
values you have to know your way around before you accept any single
figure that you see.

If we go on to Universal Insurance we find a similar
calculation, but with one interesting difference that I want to
point out.

Here you start with capital and surplus of $38.75 a
share, as shown in the report to stockholders. The unearned
premium reserve, taken at forty per cent which is standard for a
fire and marine company, would add $3.80. Marking the bonds to
market would add $2.80, giving you a total of $45.55 for the
equity, as per the Standard Statistics analysis. But here we
have the interesting item of claims against unauthorized insurance
companies, which in this case amounted to as much as $11.45 a
share. My understanding is that these are claims against Lloyds
for reinsurance of marine inderwritings. Universal Insurance
Company is largely engaged in the marine insurance field, and has
extensive dealings with Lloyds.

That marks up the equity to Best's figure of $57. But
Best in this case does not attach any footnote as to the additional
equity in the subsidiary of this company, known as Universal
Indemnity, which amounts to $3.80. When we add that we have a
final figure, which Geyer and Company use, of $60.80.

Thus in both of these cases the difference between the
first figure you find and the last figure is very substantial indeed.

I would like to add a further adjustment, which does not
appear as far as I know in any of the insurance company analyses;
and I see no reason why it should not appear. This is adjustment
in the way of a deduction. It relates to tax liability.

The investment services include in these equity
calculations the full appreciation in security prices and what
appears to be the realizable value of the unearned premium
reserves. Both of those assets, if realized, would be subject
to income tax; and I see no reason why income tax should not be

allowed for on the indicated or accrued profit in this case, as it
is in every other type of analysis which we security analysts
make.

On this basis, a correct study would make a deduction
of, say, twenty-five per cent of the appreciation in the security
portfolio for tax on capital gains; and a deduction of thirty-eight
per cent for the equity in unearned premium reserve, which is the
present rate that such equity would bear if realized. That equity
will not be realized until later, and it maynever be realized. But
if you are allowing for it, as an asset, it seems to me you should
allow for the tax that goes with it.

In the case of the North River Insurance Company, to
use one of our examples for which I have the data, the tax on
the security appreciation would amount to $1,042,000, and the
tax on the forty per cent of unearned premium would amount to
$1,260,000--a total tax of $2,300,000 or $2.90 a share. And.
therefore the calculated equity (on which all the authorities agree,
as it happens, in this case) would be reduced by about 9 per cent,
if you allow for taxes.

It may be argued that there is an off-set to that tax
liability when you are figuring liquidating values; something is
said by Best's about the extra value of the agency setup that these
companies have. These companies have a large number of agents, and
it is contended that a cash value could be realized for their
going-concern interest in the insurance business. It is conceivable
that the good-will value might offset the tax liability that I
speak of. But that seems to me an uncertain matter, while the
tax liability is quite a definite one. For that reason I would
recommend to anyone who is makingcareful calculations of the
insurance companies that they calculate the tax liabilities
involved.

Are there any questions about those items?

QUESTION: You said the reduction in tax liability
should be correlated to other companies. What companies? I mean,
what group of securities?

MR. GRAHAM: Well, I don't know whether your question
relates to my statement that when we analyze other companies we
allow for tax liability against any appreciation--

QUESTION: That's right.

MR. GRAHAM: --which we allowed for. Well, that
would be particularly true of investment companies where they are
not regulated investment companies under Supplement Q of the
Revenue Act.

QUESTION: Are there any other companies involved?

MR. GRAHAM: If you are going to calculate asset values of other companies and take their marketable securities at a price above cost, you must allow for tax thereon.

Bear this in mind: It is the standard procedure for ordinary corporations to show their securities owned at cost in their balance sheet, with a footnote or a parenthesis which indicates market value. Hence it is not necessary for them to set up in their balance sheet any allowance for tax. But if you, as an analyst, want to take the footnote figure of a higher price, you must then allow for the related tax in your calculation.

QUESTION: Referring to your allowance for thirty-eight per cent taxes against the unearned premium reserve, shouldn't you also make some provision for possible future expenses chargeable to that?

MR. GRAHAM: Well, the theory of the original forty per cent allowance is that all the expenses have been absorbed in the other sixty per cent. Of course, that may prove to be wrong, but past experience seems to justify that theory.

Are there any other questions?

QUESTION: Is that thirty to thirty-five per cent of premium reserve a standard matter--or does it vary with various companies?

MR. GRAHAM: That seems to vary with different casualty companies, according to the judgment of the statistical agencies. I should add, for completeness, that in fire reinsurance companies, which comprise another set of companies doing a reinsurance business only, the practice seems to be to allow thirty-five per cent of the premium reserves; whereas direct insuring fire companies are allowed forty per cent.

Any other questions about these techniques?

I suppose they appear to you to be quite complicated, and they are. But I imagine that once you become familiar with the issues involved they should not present an obstacle to ascertaining approximately the true stockholders' equity of a company at any time.

With this long preliminary I want to go back to the two specific companies that remain to be discussed.

Let us first consider the American Equitable Insurance Company. I have available the operating results of that company for a twenty-year period. These were calculated with considerable difficulty, and are perhaps not absolutely correct; but I think they are very close to being correct.

Between 1926 and 1945 the underwriting results showed an over-all loss of two million dollars, after allowing for forty per cent equity in unearned premiums. The investment income aggregated $6.4 million. The market appreciation, less loss on assets sold, is plus $800,000. But there were offsetting adjustments of surplus, amounting also to $800,000. The over-all gain for twenty years thus amounts to $4.4 million, against which dividends of $5.4 million were paid. All this produced was a reduction in surplus of about a million dollars in that twenty-year period.

When you analyze those results, they appear less favorable than they might at first glance. You might have assumed if a company earns four million and a half dollars over a twenty-year period, that it was pretty well. Actually I think you must say that this company did very badly indeed. Its investment income was about $6.5 million, which represented about three per cent on its average stockholders' equity. That, of course, is no tribute to the management's capability, because, having all this money to invest, it was bound to earn some relatively small rate of interest on it.

But one-third of that income was lost in the insurance business, so that in the final result the stockholders averaged about two per cent on their investment per year for a twenty-year period. The dividends exceeded that amount, and so you had a shrinkage in equity.

The security operations appear to have been almost a standoff for the twenty-year period--which is no achievement, nor is it for that matter anything to be criticized very much. However, I might point out that the Dow-Jones average at the end of 1925 stood at 157, at the end of 1945 at 192. Thus there might be some reason to expect a net gain in security operations if that end of the management had been handled with any particular skill.

With regard to the company's portfolio, you will find that it has a larger than average percentage of its total assets in common stocks. You can see certain pressures here to put money in common stocks, and to endeavor to get favorable results thereby in stock market changes, in order to offset the less than mediocre results which are shown by the ordinary operations of the business.

The result of that policy is that you have very wide fluctuations from year to year in the company's asset value. In good years it goes up sharply, and in bad years it goes down equally sharply. The stockholders' equity rose from $36.5 in December, 1936 to $52.2 in December, 1937, and declined to $27.4 in December, 1938.)

I might point out that the American Equitable Company owns about ten per cent of the stock of the American Reserve Insurance Company. That insurer, as I pointed out two weeks ago, has the worst underwriting record of all companies in the large list

of eighty which I have studied, it having made a four per cent
loss on underwriting over ten years, which is somewhat greater than
the loss of the American Equitable.

The basic problem here, as I see it, is why the stockholders as a whole are willing to keep their money in a business
that has shown such poor results for them over a period of twenty
years--and particularly poor results in the very part of their
total business which it was specifically intended to carry on,
namely, insurance underwriting.

Any number of individual stockholders have decided over
this twenty years that this is not the business for them to have
their money in, and they have sold their shares; these in turn
have been purchased by other stockholders. Those sales have been
made more or less continuously at very considerable discounts from
net asset value. The stockholders who have sold out have taken
very substantial losses, not only in the shrinkage in their equity,
but also in the additional shrinkage in market **price under** equity
which attaches to an unsuccessful business.

The question, though, is why the stockholders as a whole
do not determine that this business is not for them, and try to
take their money out of it?

There are several answers to that question, as I see it.
Perhaps other answers would occur to you. One answer, I am sure,
is that the idea has never occurred to the stockholders generally.
For stockholders take it for granted that when capital is in a
business it must stay there, and if they don't like the business
they must sell out their interest to other stockholders for whatever they can get.

I assure you, gentlemen, that there is nothing
in the principles of investment, and nothing in the laws of the
United States, which indicate that such must be the procedure of
stockholders who are, on the whole and as a body, not getting
satisfactory results on their investment.

The difficulty is not at all with the stockholders'
rights. The difficulty is with stockholders' attitudes. We
find in Wall Street no indications of any awareness of the fact that
there may be something wrong in the type of situation; and that if
there is something wrong it may be possible to correct it. I have
been speaking with regard to businesses generally which have very
unsatisfactory results over a long period of time, and from which
the stockholders as a whole could withdraw their capital without
great difficulty.

In the American Equitable case you may have an additional
situation. This company is apparently controlled by a holding
company known as Caroon and Reynolds Corp., which in turn is
identified with an insurance agency. American Equitable and three

other insurance writers are managed under contract by that insurance
agency; thus the insurance agency receives commissions, no doubt
at standard rates, on the insurance placed for those four companies.

It just happens that these four companies have about the
worst record of underwriting results for the last ten years, as
shown by the compilation which I have studied. I do not guarantee
that that compilation is right, but I have no reason to think that
it is wrong. There is one exception, namely, the American Reserve
Insurance, which has a slightly worse record; but it appears that a
substantial amount of that company is owned by American Equitable.

The problem, therefore, in the case of American Equitable
seems to be somewhat different from that of a concern in general
which has not been yielding satisfactory results to its stockholders. The problem here is how stockholders, who may in effect
be a minority group, can get relief from results of this unsatisfactory kind, which may conceivably benefit a majority group.

I would like to make a paradoxical remark about that.
Most people assume that if they are in the minority position their
position is weak as compared with being one of a widespread majority
group. I think, in actual fact, their minority position is
stronger. The reason is this: If you and thousands of other
stockholders controlled the American Equitable Insurance Company,
you could get relief by concerted action with all your fellow
stockholders, who together, have power to give you relief. That is
very simple in theory; in practice it is extremely difficult--
because for some strange reason stockholders do not wish, most
times, to help themselves, even though that may be easy to do.

If you have a minority position, on the other hand--and
the majority is running the company and perhaps getting advantages
which do not accrue to you as a minority--you have a specific right
to relief at law, as I understand the law. It may be that in this
case or in some other cases, you, as a single individual stockholder,
can obtain legal relief; whereas if you were one of the majority
you could only obtain relief by rallying most of the other "majority
stockholders" to your side.

I hope I have made this paradox clear. I will be glad
to answer any questions on it, if you have any.

QUESTION: As a practical matter, the cost of hiring
counsel and everything else would probably far offset any relief
you might obtain.

MR. GRAHAM: You mean in a typical case of this
kind?

QUESTION: Yes, a typical case. In other words, a
man has a thousand shares of stock at 16, let us say. By the time
he gets finished dragging it through the courts, he will find he

pays his lawyers more and wastes more of his own time than any relief he can get out of the thing.

MR. GRAHAM: Yes, that is a possibility which should be taken into account. It is rather serious question.

QUESTION: Doesn't the expense usually come out of a company's treasury, in a suit like that, though?

MR. GRAHAM: It is true also that the expenses on the other side are taken care of by the company's treasury, unless perhaps in some very unusual type of judgment those sums are chargeable elsewhere.

QUESTION: You can get it from a director?

MR. GRAHAM: That sum might conceivably be gotten from the directors but not probably.

QUESTION: As I understand it, under the Stock Corporation law, as at present, I think you have to have five per cent of the stock in order to bring such an action.

MR. GRAHAM: That relates to an action for damages against directors, which is not the kind of action that I was talking about. It is not my purpose here to discuss the details of legal actions by stockholders, because that certainly is outside the purview of the lecture. I merely wanted to point out that, in legal theory, a minority holder who claims that he is being harmed while the majority holders are getting other benefits has a right to assert his claim and to have it considered in court. Whereas if he was part of a majority, the court would say, "Go to your other stockholders and get them to act, because they have power to act." That is the distinction that I wished to make.

QUESTION: In the case of the American Equitable, is the management actually owner of a majority or do they merely hav a management contract and have management through proxy machinery?

MR. GRAHAM: There the question may center on the matter of working control, which is often a question of fact to be determined by courts rather than a mathematically demonstrable idea.

QUESTION: Theymay have no stock interest at all. Through the proxy machinery they may continue themselves from year to year.

MR. GRAHAM: I made the point before that here the situation is somewhat different. You have not only an agency which has these management contracts, which is not unusual, but you have a holding company as well, which owns a considerable amount of the shares of this company--about 43% of the total. So that, as you can see, it is a somewhat different picture than you suggest.

Are there any other questions? I would like to get away from matters of law for a number of reasons, one of which is that I am not a lawyer; but I did want to get the general picture before you.

Now, we turn to the New Amsterdam Casualty case, which is interesting for a completely different set of reasons, as I pointed out in the previous lecture. Here you have a very large discount in price from break-up value, but instead of having an unprofitable company, you have one which, over the years, has shown very good results indeed. Instead of having the stockholders suffering from what might be called a certain waste of assets-- in the sense of a business which is carried on for years on a relatively losing basis--you have exactly the opposite: The stockholder is suffering from an undue desire by management to gather together and retain all the assets possible and to give out as little as they decently can to the stockholders. I think the contrast in the two cases is very extraordinary, and it deserves some careful thinking on your side. For it shows that the stockholders' interests are affected by developments and policies of a very diverse nature, and that a stockholder can suffer from failure to pay out earnings, when they are realized, nearly as much as he suffers from the failure to realize earnings.

Now, that will be vigorously denied by corporate managements, who insist that as long as the money is made and is retained in the treasury the stockholder does not possibly suffer and he can only gain. I think you gentlemen are better qualified than anyone else to be the judge of that very question. Is it true that the outside stockholder invariably benefits from the retention of earnings in the business, as distinct from the payment of a fair return on the value of his equity in the form of dividends? I believe that Wall Street experience shows clearly that the best treatment for stockholders is the payment to them of fair and reasonable dividends in relation to the company's earnings and in relation to the true value of the security, as measured by any ordinary tests based on earning power or assets.

In my view the New Amsterdam Casualty case is a very vivid example of how security holders can suffer through failure to pay adequate dividends. This company, as I remarked two weeks ago, has been paying a $1 dividend, which is the same amount as paid by the other two companies. Its average earnings have been very much higher. For the five years 1941-5, the earnings are shown to have averaged $4.33, after taxes, as against which their maximum dividend has been $1 per annum.

You will recall that the North River Company during that period earned an average of $1.12, one quarter as much, and paid the same dividend of one dollar. And the American Equitable, which earned an average of nine cents in those five years, also paid one dollar.

If the New Amsterdam Company had been paying a dividend commensurate with its earnings and its assets, both, there is no doubt in my mind but that the stockholders would have benefited in two major ways: First, they would have received an adequate return on their money, which is a thing of very great moment in the case of the average stockholder, and secondly they would have enjoyed a better market price for their stock.

It turns out that we have an extraordinarily pat comparative example here in the form of another casualty company, called the U. S. Fidelity and Guaranty. This pursues an almost identical line of business, and has almost identical earnings and almost identical assets, per share, as has New Amsterdam. But it happens to pay two dollars a share in dividends instead of one dollar a share, and so it has been selling recently at about 45; whereas New Amsterdam stock has been selling at somewhere around 26 to 28.

The difference in results to the stockholder between paying a reasonable and fair dividend and paying a niggardly dividend is made as manifest as it can be by these contrasting examples.

You may ask: What is the reason advanced by the management for failure to pay a more substantial dividend, when it appears that the price of the stock and the stockholders' dividend return both suffer so much from the present policy?

You will find, if you talk to the management on the subject, that they will give you three reasons for their dividend policy; and if you have done similar missionary work over a period of time, the arguments will sound strangely familiar to you.

The first reason they give you is conservatism--that is, it is desirable, and in the interest of the stockholders, to be as conservative as possible. It is a good thing to be conservative, of course. The real question at issue is, can a company be too conservative? Would the stockholders be better off, for example, if they received no dividend at all, rather than one dollar--which would be carrying the conservatism to its complete extreme? I believe that experience shows that conservatism of this kind can be carried to the point of seriously harming the stockholders' interest.

The second reason that you will get from the company--and you will get it from every other company in the same position--is that theirs is a very special business and it has special hazards; and it is necessary to be much more careful in conducting this business than in conducting the average business or any other one that you might mention. In this particular case they would point out also that the results for the year 1946 have been unsatisfactory, and that the current situation is by no means good.

Since every business is a special business, it seems to me that the argument more or less answers itself. You would have to conclude that there would be no principles by which the stockholders can determine suitable treatment for themselves, if it is to be assumed that each business is so different from every other that no general principles can be applied to it.

With regard to the statement that the 1946 results have been poor, it happens that if you analyze them in the usual fashion you would find that even in a bad year like 1946 the New Amsterdam Casualty Company appeared to earn on the order of two dollars and a half a share. Therefore it could well have afforded a larger dividend than one dollar, even if you took the one-year results alone, which it is by no means the proper standard to follow. Dividend policy should be based upon average earnings in the past and upon expected average earnings in the future.

It will be pointed out that some companies have been having difficulties in the insurance business in the last two years, and for that reason it is very desirable that conservatism be followed. We all know there have been some very unprofitable insurance concerns, and some have been profitable. To say that stockholders of profitable businesses cannot get reasonable dividends because there are some unprofitable or some possibly shaky companies in the field, I would call rather irrelevant.

The third argument--and this is especially interesting, I believe, because it comes down to the essence of stockholders' procedures and rights--is that the stockholders do not understand the problems of the business as well as the management of a company. Therefore it is little short of impertinence for the stockholders to suggest that they know better than the management what is the proper policy to follow in their interest.

Of course, the trouble with that argument is that it prove too much. It would mean that regardless of what issue was raised, the stockholders should never express themselves, and should never dare to have an opinion contrary to the management's. I think you would all agree that the principle of stockholders' control over managements would be completely vitiated if you assume that managements _always_ knew what was the best thing to do and always acted in the stockholders' interest on every point.

I want to say, with regard to the New Amsterdam Company-- since in this course we have been mentioning names right along, for the sake of vividness--two things: First, I should have started by saying that my investment company has an interest in the New Amsterdam Casualty Company, and I have had a dispute with the management as to proper dividend policy. I want to say that, because you may believe that this presentation has been biased-- and you are perfectly free to form that conclusion if you wish. You should be warned of the possibility of bias. My belief, of course, is that the statements made fairly represent the issues in the case.

The second point I want to make very emphatically is that the New Amsterdam Casualty Company is extremely well managed by very capable people of the highest character, and that the issue that arises here is not one of self-interest on the part of the management, or lack of ability, but solely the question of dividend policy, and its impact on the stockholders' interest.

The solution of this problem of the stockholders' interest in the New Amsterdam case, and many others, is not easy to predict. As I see it, after a good deal of thought, analysis and argument on the subject, you need in these cases a long process of stockholder education, so that they will come to think for themselves and act for themselves. Whether that will ever be realized I don't know; but I am very hopeful that people in Wall Street might play a part in giving stockholders sound and impartial guidance in regard to the holdings that they have, as well as to the securities which they might think of buying or selling.

Let me summarize this analysis of the insurance companies in a few words.

The insurance business appears to be generally unsatisfactory to stockholders in terms of the things that interest them most, namely, dividends and market price. The reasons for this fact are different in different cases, and hence there is need for discriminating analysis of results and for weighing corporate policies with a careful mind.

Thirdly, the entire industry, in its history, shows a development away from the community of interest between management and stockholders which existed twenty years ago and which made for very satisfactory results from everybody's angle. The development has been in the direction of a sharp clash of attitude and interest between the intelligent and alert stockholder on the one hand, and entrenched managements on the other.

I think you will find that the insurance company industry supplies an excellent area for a beginning in the development of a real reform in stockholder-management relations.

Some of you may have read Mr. Caffrey's address recently--he is the chairman of the SEC--in which he called for more alert action by stockholders and a better opportunity to be given to stockholders by corporations to express themselves.

Here in the insurance field I thin a great deal of advantage would accrue to the stockholders if, first, the issues which affect their interest were clearly and fairly drawn; secondly, if the stockholders are fully informed about these issues; and thirdly and most of all, if the stockholders could possibly get some impartial and competent guidance, some sound advice, with respect to what they should do in their own interest.

It may be that this analysis, which has taken us two hours, is completely wrong. It may be that I have stressed elements which either have been unfairly presented to you or which ignore other and offsetting elements. That is always a possibility in the abstract. But the main thing about this matter is not so much who is right or who is wrong; but rather that you have a condition which is extraordinary--one which requires attention and careful thinking and maybe action--and which is completely ignored by the people who are mostly interested--namely, the owners of these companies.

The first thing that is necessary is to make the owners of the companies aware that they have an issue and a problem. After that, I think the question of the rights and the wrongs of the problem can be developed in the proper forums, and I certainly hope the matter will get a very thorough-going consideration.

I have two minutes left and I think there must be some questions.

QUESTION: Would you care to comment on the abuse by managements of insurance companies in dumping securities on portfolios of insurance companies?

MR. GRAHAM: I believe that abuse existed many years ago. I see no indication of its existing at the present time, or in recent years.

QUESTION: It is an easy way to make an underwriting commission on a new issue, and you know darn well that you can place it because you yourself are both seller and buyer.

MR. GRAHAM: I think that is true in theory, but my own impression is that if it does exist as an abuse, it is a very minor abuse. It is not a major factor now.

QUESTION: How much of this apparent conservatism is a carry-over of the days of the early 'thirties when they took heavy security losses? Do you think they are afraid that will happen again?

MR. GRAHAM: Yes, the conservatism of New Amsterdam has a great deal to do with that. If you speak to the management of this company and perhaps other companies, they will tell you that they went through a terrible time in the 1930's; they were compelled to pass the dividend and they don't want to go through it again--which is perfectly proper statement to make. But that doesn't mean that they should not pay a reasonable dividend to their stockholders.

QUESTION: Isn't there a penalty tax the companies have to pay to the Government if they don't pay out seventy per cent in dividends?

MR. GRAHAM: There is some question as to whether
that applies to insurance companies or not. As a statutory matter
it does apply--that is, the insurance companies are also subject
to Section 102 relating to "improper accumulation of surplus."
As a practical matter, I imagine it is relatively easy for them
to show that the money can be used in the business. They do have
to file that tax report, which simply explains why they have failed
to pay as much as seventy per cent of their earnings in dividends.

QUESTION: Wouldn't the liquidating value of this
New Amsterdam Company back in 1940 be about $26? And if that is
true, how did it move up so rapidly? I looked at the portfolio.
Now it seems very conservative. Have they changed their policy?

MR. GRAHAM: Not recently. Many years ago they had
common stocks of considerable amounts. They have not had common
stocks for many years. The increase in value is due to the simple
fact that they earned a great deal of money and paid out a very
small part of it.

QUESTION: In those six years?

MR. GRAHAM: In those six years the average earnings
were more than four dollars a share.

QUESTION: We were talking about the amount you
consider reasonable out of earnings. Do you make any difference
between the investment account and the underwriting account, one
from the other?

MR. GRAHAM: No. They, I believe, should be lumped
together because they both are standard parts of the company's
business. The income that is not to be distributed, presumably,
would be profit through the increased value of securities owned,
which everybody agrees is not a normal type of income.

QUESTION: Are there any large stockholders in that
management group that might be interested in not receiving dividends
for tax reasons?

MR. GRAHAM: It is true, I think, that almost any large
stockholder, who is on the inside of a company, has a bias against
a large dividend as compared with a small one, because he pays a
considerable tax on the dividend. He does not need the dividend to
establish the value for him, because his value is separately
established by the fact that he is on the inside of the company
and controls it. The position of the inside stockholder in that
respect is completely different from that of the outside stockholder.

QUESTION: Are there any in New Amsterdam Casualty?

MR. GRAHAM: There may be some.

QUESTION: Has the New Amsterdam Company had any
more pronounced growth trend than the U. S. Fidelity Company that
I believe you mentioned, or not?

MR. GRAHAM: I believe that the rate in increase
in premiums has been about the same.

QUESTION: What is the usual dividend for a company
in that condition?

MR. GRAHAM: My feeling is that the company should
pay not less than four per cent on the fair value of its stock,
provided the earnings will permit such a payment with a fair
margin. In this case it would be about two dollars a share.

QUESTION: In relation to per cent of earnings,
do you care to make any generalization that a company in good
financial condition should pay out at least fifty per cent of
its earnings?

MR. GRAHAM: I would presume that at least fifty
per cent should be paid out.

QUESTION: How much more than fifty per cent?

MR. GRAHAM: I have no worthwhile opinion on that.

That will be all for today.

Lecture No. 10   February 25, 1947

CURRENT PROBLEMS IN SECURITY ANALYSIS

By
Benjamin Graham
****

MR. GRAHAM: Ladies and gentlemen, this is the last of our series of lectures. I hope that you will have found it as enjoyable and stimulating to listen to them as I have found it in preparing them.

The final talk is going to be something of departure, for it will address itself to speculation--speculation in relation to security analysis.

Speculation, I imagine, is a theme almost as popular as love; but in both cases most of the comments made are rather trite and not particularly helpful. (Laughter)

In discussing speculation in the context of this lecture it will be my effort to bring out some of the less obvious aspects of this important element in finance and in your own work.

There are three main points that I would like to make in this hour. The first is that speculative elements are of some importance in nearly all the work of the security analyst, and of considerable importance in part of his work; and that the over-all weight and significance of speculation has been growing over the past thirty years.

The second point is that there is a real difference between intelligent and unintelligent speculation, and that the methods of security analysis may often be of value in distinguishing between the two kinds of speculation.

My third point is that, despite the two foregoing statements, I believe that the present attitude of security analysts toward speculation is in the main unsound and unwholesome. The basic reason therefor is that our emphasis tends to be placed on the rewards of successful speculation rather than on our capacity to speculate successfully.

There is a great need, consequently, for a careful, self-examining critique of the security analyst as speculator, and that means in turn a self-critique by the so-called typical investor, acting as speculator.

First, what do we mean by speculation? There is a chapter in our book on Security Analysis which is devoted to the

distinctions between investment and speculation. I don't wish to
repeat that material beyond recalling to you our concluding
definition, which reads as follows:

> "An investment operation is one which, on thorough
> analysis, promises safety of principal and a satisfactory
> return. Operations not meeting these requirements are
> speculative."

That is a very brief reference to speculation. We could
amplify it a bit by saying that in speculative operations a
successful result cannot be predicated on the processes of
security analysis. That doesn't mean that speculation can't be
successful, but it simply means you can't be a successful speculator
in individual cases merely by following our methods of security
analysis.

Speculative operations are all concerned with changes in
price. In some cases the emphasis is on price changes alone, and
in other cases the emphasis is on changes in value which are
expected to give rise to changes in price. I think that is a
rather important classification of speculative operations. It
is easy to give examples.

If at the beginning of 1946 a person bought U. S. Steel
at around 80, chiefly because he believed that in the latter part
of bull markets the steel stocks tend to have a substantial move,
that would clearly be a speculative operation grounded primarily
on an opinion as to price changes, and without any particular
reference to value.

On the other hand, a person who bought Standard Gas and
Electric, $4 preferred, sometime in 1945, at a low price,--say at
$4 a share--because he thought the plan which provided for its
extinction was likely to be changed, was speculating undoubtedly.
But there his motive was related to an analysis of value--or
rather to an expected change of value--which, as it happened, was
realized spectacularly in the case of the Standard Gas and Electric
Preferred issue.

I think it is clear to you that in a converse sense
nearly all security operations which are based essentially on
expected changes, whether they are of price or of value, must be
regarded as speculative, and distinguished from investment.

In our chapter on speculation and investment we discussed
the concept of the speculative component in a price. You remember
we pointed out that a security might sell at a price which reflected
in part its investment value and in part an element which should be
called speculative.

The example we gave back in 1939-1940, with considerable
trepidation, was that of General Electric. We intentionally picked

out the highest-grade investment issue we could find to illustrate the element of speculation existing in it. Of the price of 38, which it averaged in 1939, we said the analyst might conclude that about $25 a share represented the investment component and as much as $13 a share represented the speculative component. Hence in this very high-grade issue about one-third of the average price in a more or less average market represents a speculative appraisal.

That example, which showed how considerable was the speculative component in investment securities, I think is pretty typical of security value developments since World War I. I believe it justifies and explains the first point that I wish to make, namely, that speculative elements have become more and more important in the work of the analyst. I think only people who have been in Wall Street for a great many years can appreciate the change in the status of investment common stocks that took place in the last generation, and the extent to which speculative considerations have obtruded themselves in all common stocks.

When I came down to the Street in 1914, an investment issue was not regarded as speculative, and it wasn't speculative. Its price was based primarily upon an established dividend. It fluctuated relatively little in ordinary years. And even in years of considerable market and business changes the price of investment issues did not go through very wide fluctuations. It was quite possible for the investor, if he wished, to disregard price changes completely, considering only the soundness and dependability of his dividend return, and let it go at that--perhaps every now and then subjecting his issue to a prudent scrutiny.

That fact is illustrated on the blackboard by taking the rather extreme case of the Consolidated Gas Company, now Consolidated Edison Company, during the years of the first postwar boom and depression--namely, 1919-1923. These vicissitudes really affected the company quite severely; for you will notice that its earnings suffered wide fluctuations, and got down in 1920 to only $1.40 a share for the hundred-dollar par value stock. Yet during that period it maintained its established dividend of $7 and its price fluctuation was comparatively small for a major market swing--that is, it covered a range of 106 down to 71.

If we go back to the years 1936-1938, which in the textbooks is now referred to as a mere "recession" that lasted for a year, we find that Consolidated Edison Company, with no changes in earnings to speak of, had extraordinarily wide changes in price. During the year 1937 alone it declined from about 50 to 21, and the following year went down to 17. During that period it actually raised its dividend, and its earnings were very stable. (See comparative data in the following table.)

T A B L E

RECORD OF CONSOLIDATED EDISON (Consolidated Gas)

IN SELECTED YEARS

(Per Share figures)

Year	Earnings	Dividend	Price Range
1919	$4.10	$7	106--80
1920	1.40	7	94--71
1921	6.80	7	95--73
1922	10.16	7.50	146--86
(New stock)			
1936	2.33	1.75	48--27
1937	2.19	2.00	50--21
1938	2.09	2.00	34--17

- -

The much wider fluctuations in investment common stocks
that have come about since World War I have made it practically
impossible for buyers of common stocks to disregard price changes.
It would be extremely unwise--and hypocritical--for anybody to buy
a list of common stocks and say that he was interested only in his
dividend return and cared nothing at all about price changes.

The problem is not whether price changes should be
disregarded--because clearly they should not be--but rather in what
way can the investor and the security analyst deal intelligently
with the price changes which take place.

I would like to go back for a moment to our statement
that in the case of General Electric a considerable portion of
the price in 1939 reflected a speculative component. That arises
from the fact that investors have been willing to pay so much for
so-called quality, and so much for so-called future prospects,
on the average, that they have themselves introduced serious
speculative elements into common stock valuations. These elements
are bound to create fluctuations in their own attitude, because
quality and prospects are psychological factors. The dividend,
of course, is not a psychological factor; it is more or less of
a fixed datum. Matters of the former kind--I am speaking now of
prospects and quality--are subject to wide changes in the
psychological attitude of the people who buy and sell stocks. Thus
we find that General Electric will vary over a price range almost
as wide as that of any secondary stock belonging in more or less
the same price class.

Going ahead from 1939 to 1946, we find that General
Electric declined from 44½ down to 21½ and came back again to
52 in 1946, and has since declined to 33, or thereabouts. These
are wide fluctuations. I think they justify my statement that a
very considerable part of the price of General Electric must be

regarded as speculative and perhaps temporary.

I think also you might say that the pure investment valuation of $25 for General Electric could be said to be justified by the sequel, since there were opportunities both in 1941 and 1942 to buy the stock at those levels. It is also true that the price movement of General Electric was not as favorable between 1939 and 1946 as that of other stocks, and I think that reflects the rather over-emphasized speculative element that appeared in General Electric before World War II.

Speculative components may enter into bonds and preferred stocks as well as into common stocks. But a high-grade bond, almost by definition, has practically no speculative component. In fact, if you thought it had a large speculative component, you would not buy it for investment nor would you call it high grade. But there is one important factor to be borne in mind here. A rise in interest rates may cause a substantial decline in the price of a very good bond. But even in that event a high-grade bond may be valued on its amortized basis throughout the period that it runs, and the price fluctuations could therefore be ignored by a conventional treatment of value. As most of you know, that is exactly what is done in the insurance company valuation methods which we were discussing recently. High-grade bonds are valued from year to year on an amortized basis, without reference to price fluctuations.

It may be a pleasant thing for the security analyst to get away from the speculative components that are found chiefly in common stocks and which are so troublesome, and to concentrate on the more responsive and more controllable elements in bond analysis. Wall Street, I believe, has improved very greatly its technique of bond analysis since 1929. But it is one of the ironies of life that just when you have got something really under control it is no longer as important as it used to be. I think we must all admit that bond analysis plays a very much smaller part in the work of the analyst and in the activities of the investor than it used to. The reason is perfectly obvious: The greater portion of bond investments now consist of U. S. Government bonds, which do not require or lend themselves to a formal bond analysis.

While it is true that for the minor portion of corporate bonds that remain you can go through all the motions of careful bond analysis, even that is likely to be somewhat frustrating. For I am sure that a really competent bond analyst is almost certain to come up with the conclusion in nearly every case that the typical buyer would be better off with a Government bond than with a well-entrenched corporate security. The purchase of these corporate securities in the present market is a kind of pro forma affair by the large institutions who, for semi-political reasons, desire to have corporate bonds in their portfolios as well as Government bonds. The result is that the wide field of bond analysis, which used to be so important to and so rewarding to the bond investor, must now, I think, be written down pretty far in terms of practical interest.

So much, then, for my first point: that willy-nilly we
security analysts find that more and more significance attaches
to speculative elements in the securities that we are turning our
attention to.

On the second point, which relates to the analyst's role
in distinguishing intelligent from unintelligent speculation, I
would like to treat that matter chiefly by some examples.

I have picked out four low-price securities, which I
think would illustrate the different kinds of results which an
analyst may get from dealing with primarily speculative securities.
These are, on the one hand, Alleghany Corp. Common, which sold at
the end of the month at 5, and Graham-Paige Common, which sold at
5; and, on the other hand, General Shareholdings, which sold at 4,
and Electric Bond and Share $6 Preferred "Stubs", which could be
bought yesterday at the equivalent of 3.

When we first look at these securities, they all seem
pretty much the same--namely, four speculative issues, which they
certainly are. But a deeper examination by a security analyst
would reveal a quite different picture in the two pairs of cases.

In the case of General Shareholdings we have the following:
This is the common stock of an investment company, which has 21½
million dollars of total assets, with senior claims of 12 million
dollars, and a balance of about 9½ million for the common. The
common is selling for $6,400,000 in the market. That means that
in General Shareholdings you have both a market discount from
the apparent present value of the stock and an opportunity to
participate in a highly leveraged situation. For if you pay $6.4
million for the common stock, you are paying only thirty per cent
of the gross asset value; and consequently every ten per cent of
increase in total asset value would mean a thirty per cent increase
in the book value of the common.

Furthermore, you are practically immune from any danger
of serious corporate trouble; because the greater portion of the
senior securities--in fact, five-sixths of it--is represented by
a preferred stock on which dividends do not have to be paid and
on which there is no maturity date.

Consequently, in the General Shareholdings case, you have
that typically attractive speculative combination of (a) a low-price
"ticket of entry" into a fairly large situation; and (b) instead of
paying more than the mathematical value of your ticket, you are
paying less; and (c), if you assume that wide fluctuations are
likely to occur in both directions over the years, you stand to
gain more than you can lose from these fluctuations.

So much for General Shareholdings, viewed analytically.

By contrast, if you go to Alleghany Corporation at 5,
although it seems at first to be a somewhat similar situation--

namely an interest in an investment company portfolio--you find
the mathematical picture completely different. At the end of
1945 the company had about 85 million dollars of assets, and against
it there were 125 million dollars of claims in the form of bonds
and preferred stocks, including unpaid dividends. Thus the common
stock was about 40 million dollars "under water." Yet at 5 you
would be paying 22 million dollars for your right to participate
in any improved value for this 85 million of assets,--after the
prior claims were satisfied.

       The security analyst would say that there is plenty of
leverage in that situation, of course; but you are paying so much
for it, and you are so far removed from an actual realizable
profit, that it would be an unintelligent speculation.

       The fact of the matter is you would need a 70% increase
in the value of the Allegheny portfolio merely to be even with
the market price of the common as far as asset value coverage is
concerned. In the case of General Shareholdings, if you had a
seventy per cent increase in the value of its portfolio, you would
have an asset value of about $15 a share for the common, as against
a market price of around 4.

       Thus, from the analytical standpoint, while Allegheny
and General Shareholdings represent approximately the same
general picture, there is a very wide quantitative disparity between
the two. One turns out to be an intelligent and the other an
unintelligent speculation.

       Passing now to Graham-Paige at five dollars, we find
another type of situation. Here the public is paying about $24
million for a common stock which represents about $8 million
of asset value, most of which is in Kaiser-Fraser stock. This
you can buy if you want in the open market, instead of having to
pay three times as much for it. The rest of the price represents
an interest in $3 million of assets in the farm equipment business--
which may prove profitable, as any business may be profitable.
The only weakness to that is that there is no record of profitable
operations here, and you are paying a great many millions of
dollars merely for some possibilities. That, in turn, would be
regarded as an unintelligent speculation by the security analyst.

       Let us move on now to the Electric Bond and Share Stubs,
which I shall describe briefly. They represent what you would
have left if you had bought Electric Bond and Share Preferred at
$73 yesterday and had then received $70 a share that is now to be
distributed. What remains is an interest in a possible $10
payment, your claim to which is to be adjudicated by the SEC and
the courts. That $10 represents the premium above par to which
Electric Bond and Share Preferred would be entitled if it were
called for redemption. The question to be decided is whether the
call price, the par value, or some figure in between should govern
in this case.

It should be obvious, I think, that that is a speculative situation. You may get $10 a share out of it for your $3, and you may get nothing at all, or you may get something in between. But it is not a speculative operation that eludes the techniques of the security analyst. He has means of examining into the merits of the case and forming an opinion based upon his skill, his experience, and the analogies which he can find in other public utility dissolutions.

If we were to assume that the Electric Bond and Share Stubs have a fifty-fifty chance of getting the ten-dollar premium, then he would conclude that at $3 a share they are an intelligent speculation. For the mathematics indicates that, in several such operations, you would make more than you would lose in the aggregate. These examples lead us, therefore, to what I would call a mathematical or statistical formulation of the relationship between intelligent speculation and investment. The two, actually, are rather closely allied.

Intelligent speculation presupposes at least that the mathematical possibilities are not against the speculation, basing the measurement of these odds on experience and the careful weighing of relevant facts.

This would apply, for example, to the purchase of common stocks at anywhere within the range of value that we find by our appraisal method. If you go back for a moment to our appraisal of American Radiator, you may recall that in our fifth lecture we went through a lot of calculations and came out with the con- clusion that American Radiator was apparently worth between $15 and $18 a share. If we assume that that job was well done, we could draw these conclusions. The investment value of American Radiator is about fifteen dollars; between 15 and 18 you would be embarking on what might be called an intelligent speculation, because it would be justified by your appraisal of the speculative factors in the case. If you went beyond the top range of $18 you would be going over into the field of unintelligent speculation.

If the probabilities, as measured by our mathematical test, are definitely in favor of the speculation, then we can transform these separate intelligent speculations into investment by the simple device of diversification. That, I think, is a clue to the most successful and rewarding treatment of speculation in Wall Street. The idea, in fine, is simply to get the odds on your side by processes of skillful, experienced calculation.

Going back to our Electric Bond and Share example, if we really are skillful in our evaluation of the possibilities here, and reach this conclusion of a fifty-fifty possibility, then we could consider Electric Bond and Share Stubs as part of an investment operation consisting of, say, ten such ventures of a diversified character. For in ten such operations you would get $50 back for an investment of $30, if you have average luck. That is, you would get $10 each on five of them and you would get nothing on another five, and your aggregate return would be $50.

Very little has been done in Wall Street to work out these arithmetical aspects of intelligent speculation based on favorable odds. In fact, the very language may be strange to most of you. Yet it oughtn't to be. If we are allowed to commit some misdemeanor by making some mild comparisons between Wall Street and horce-racing, the thought might occur to some of us that the intelligent operator in Wall Street would try to follow the technique of the bookmaker rather than the technique of the man who bets on the horses. Further, if we assume that a very consi- derable amount of Wall Street activity must inevitably have elements of chance in it, then the sound idea would be to measure these chances as accurately as you can, and play the game ih the direction of having the odds on your side.

Therefore, quite seriously, I would recommend to this group, and to any other, that the mathematical odds of speculation in various types of Wall Street operations would provide a full and perhaps a profitable field of research for students.

Let us return for a moment to Alleghany Common and Graham-Paige Common, which we characterized as unintelligent speculation from the analyst's viewpoint. Is not this a dangerous kind of statement for us to make? Last year Graham-Paige sold as high as 16, and Alleghany as high as $8\frac{1}{4}$, against the current figure of 5. It must be at least conceivable that their purchase today might turn out very well, either because (a) the abilities of Mr. Young or Mr. Fraser will create real value where none or little now exists, or (b) the stocks will have a good speculative "move," regardless of value.

Both of these possibilities exist, and the analyst cannot afford to ignore them. Yet he may stick to his guns in character- izing both stocks as unintelligent speculations, because his exper- ience teaches him that this type of speculation does not work out well on the average. One reason is that the people who buy this kind of stock at 5 are more likely to buy more at 10 than to sell it. Consequently, they usually show losses in the end, even though there may have been a chance in the interim to sell out to even less intelligent buyers. Thus, in the end, the criterion of both intelligent and unintelligent speculation rests on the results of diversified experience.

When I come to my third point I am going to indicate how very different are the ordinary and customary attitudes toward speculative risk in Wall Street than those we have been discussing. But I think I ought to pause here for a minute, since I finished my second point, and see if there are some questions to be asked on this exposition.

QUESTION: By diversification, as in the case of Electric Bond and Share Stubs--you wouldn't concentrate on ten

situations similar in the way of redemption of preferred. You would
want to diversify with Electric Bond and Share stocks and General
Shareholdings, and some others; entirely different situations?

MR. GRAHAM: Yes, the approach is not based on the
character of the operation, but only on the mathematical odds
which you have been able to determine to your own satisfaction.
It doesn't make any difference what you are buying, whether a bond
or a stock or in what field, if you are reasonably well satisfied
that the odds are in your favor. They are all of equal attractiveness, and they all belong equally in your diversification. You
make a further sound point, and that is that you are not really
diversifying if you went into ten Electric Bond and Share
situations--all substantially the same. You would not really be
diversifying, because that is practically the same thing as buying
ten shares of Electric Bond and Share instead of buying one share
of each; since the same factors would apply to all of them. That
point is well taken. For real diversification, you must be sure
that the factors that make for success or failure differ in one
case from another.

Are there any other questions about that?

QUESTION: As for that fifty-fifty chance, why
didn't you come up with sixty-forty--in Bond and Share? I don't
see how you can be so mathematically precise.

MR. GRAHAM: Of course you are right in saying that,
and I am glad you raised the point. This is not something that
admits of a Euclidean demonstration. But you can reach the
conclusion that the chances are considerably better than seven
to three, let us say--which are the odds that are involved in your
purchase--without being exactly sure whether they are fifty-fifty
or sixty-forty. Broadly speaking, you simply say you think the
chances are at least even in your favor, and you let it go at
that. But that is enough for the purpose. You don't have to be
any more accurate for practical action.

(Now, bear in mind I am not trying to imply here that
the figure given is necessarily my conclusion as to what the odds
in the Bond and Share are. Any of you are perfectly competent
to study that situation and draw a conclusion based upon what has
taken place in other utility redemptions. I am only using the
Stubs for purposes of illustration. I should point out that the
market does not seem to be very intelligent in paying the same
price for the $5 Preferred Stubs as for the $6 Preferred Stubs.)

The final subject that I have is the current attitude
of security analysts toward speculation. It seems to me that
Wall Street analysts show an extraordinary combination of sophis-
tication and naivete in their attitude toward speculation. They
recognize, and properly so, that speculation is an important part
of their environment. We all know that if we follow the speculative

crowd we are going to lose money in the long run. Yet, somehow
or other, we find ourselves very often doing just that. It is
extraordinary how frequently security analysts and the crowd are
doing the same thing. In fact, I must say I can't remember any
case in which they weren't. (Laughter.)

It reminds me of the story you all know of the oil man
who went to Heaven and asked St. Peter to let him in. St. Peter
said,"Sorry, the oil men's area here is all filled up, as you
can see by looking through the gate." The man said, "That's
too bad, but do you mind if I just say four words to them?" And
St. Peter said, "Sure." So the man shouts good and loud, "Oil
discovered in hell!" Whereupon all the oil men begin trooping out
of Heaven and making a beeline for the nether regions. Then
St. Peter said, "That was an awfully good stunt. Now there's
plenty of room, come right in." The oil man scratches his head
and says, "I think I'll go with the rest of the boys. There may
be some truth in that rumor after all." (Laughter.)

I think that is the way we behave, very often, in the
movements of the stock market. We know from experience that we
are going to end up badly, but somehow "there may be some truth
in the rumor ," so we go along with the boys.

For some reason or other, all security analysts in Wall
Street are supposed to have an opinion on the future of the market.
Many of our best analytical brains are constantly engaged in the
effort to forecast the movement of prices. I don't want to fight
out the battle over again here, as to whether their activity is
sound or not. But I would like to make one observation on this
subject.

The trouble with market forecasting is not that it is
done by unintelligent and unskillful people. Quite to the
contrary, the trouble is that it is done by so many really expert
people that their efforts constantly neutralize each other, and end
up almost exactly in zero.

The market already reflects, almost at every time,
everything that the experts can reliably say about its future.
Everything in addition which they say is therefore unreliable,
and it tends to be right just about half the time. If people
analyzing the market would engage in the proper kind of self-
criticism, I am sure they would realize that they are chasing a
will-o'-the-wisp.

Reading recently the biography of Balzac, I recalled
that novel of his called, The Search for the Absolute, which some
of you may have read. In it a very intelligent doctor spends all
his time looking for something which would be wonderful if he
found it, but which he never finds. The reward for being
consistently right on the market is enormous, of course, and that
is why we are all tempted. But I think you must agree with me that

there is no sound basis for believing that anyone can be constantly
right in forecasting the stock market. In my view it is a great
logical and practical mistake for security analysts to waste their
time on this pursuit.

Market forecasting, of course, is essentially the same
as market "timing." On that subject let me say that the only
principle of timing that has ever worked well consistently is to
buy common stocks at such times as they are cheap by analysis,
and to sell them at such times as they are dear, or at least no
longer cheap, by analysis.

That sounds like timing; but when you consider it you
will see that it is not really timing at all but rather the
purchase and sale of securities by the method of valuation.
Essentially, it requires no opinion as to the future of the
market; because if you buy securities cheap enough, your position
is sound, even if the market should continue to go down. And if
you sell the securities at a fairly high price you have done the
smart thing, even if the market should continue to go up.

Therefore, at the conclusion of this course, I hope you
will permit me to make as strong a plea as I can to you security
analysts to divorce yourselves from stock market analysis. Don't
try to combine the two--security analysis and market analysis--
plausible as this effort appears to many of us; because the end-
product of that combination is almost certain to be contradiction
and confusion.

On the other hand, I should greatly welcome an effort
by security analysts to deal intelligently with speculative
operations. To my mind the prerequisite here is for the quantitative approach, which is based on the calculation of the probabilities in each case, and a conclusion that the odds are strongly
in favor of the operation's success. It is not necessary that
this calculation be completely dependable in each instance, and
certainly not mathematically precise, but only that it be made
with a fair degree of knowledge and skill. The law of averages
will take care of minor errors and of the many individual disappointments which are inherent in speculation by its very
defintion.

It is a great mistake to believe that a speculation has
been unwise if you lose money at it. That sounds like an obvious
conclusion, but actually it is not true at all. A speculation is
unwise only if it is made on insufficient study and by poor
judgment. I recall to those of you who are bridge players the
emphasis that the bridge experts place on playing a hand right
rather than on playing it successfully. Because, as you know,
if you play it right you are going to make money and if you play
it wrong you lose money--in the long run.

There is a beautiful little story, that I suppose most
of you have heard, about the man who was the weaker bridge player

of the husband-and-wife team. It seems he bid a grand slam, and
at the end he said very triumphantly to his wife, "I saw you
making faces at me all the time, but you notice I not only bid
this grand slam but I made it. What can you say about that?"
And his wife replied very dourly, "If you had played it right you
would have lost it." (Laughter.)

There is a great deal of that in Wall Street, particularly
in the field of speculation, when you are trying to do it by
careful calculation. In some cases the thing will work out badly.
But that is simply part of the game. If it was bound to work out
rightly, it wouldn't be a speculation   at all, and there
wouldn't be the opportunities of profit that inhere in
sound speculation. It seems to me that is axiomatic.

I would like to pause here for some questions on this
matter of the security analyst's attitude toward speculation. I
have given a lot of thought to it. I know something of the practica
problems that confront the security analyst who wants to act
logically all the time, and who wants to confine himself only to
that area of financial work in which he can say with confidence
that his work and his conclusions are reasonably dependable. The
analysts all complain to me that they can't do that because they are
expected by their customers and their employers to do something
else, to give them off-the-cuff speculative judgments and market
opinions. One of these days I am sure the security analysts will
divide themselves completely from the market analysts.

It would be very nice to have a two-year trial period in
which the market analysts would keep track of what they have
accomplished through the period and security analysts would keep
track of what they have accomplished. I think it would be rather
easy to tell in advance who would turn in the better score. That
is really the pay-off. I think that eventually the employers and
the customers will come to the conclusion that it is better to let
the security analysts be security analysts--which they know how
to do--and not other kinds of things, particularly market analysts,
which they don't know how to do and they will never know how to do.

I would like to make some final observations, relating to
a long period of time, as to what has happened to the conduct of
business in Wall Street.

If you can throw your mind, as I can, as far back as
1914, you would be struck by some extraordinary differences in
Wall Street then and today. In a great number of things, the
improvement has been tremendous. The ethics of Wall Street are
very much better. The competence and intelligence of the people
in it are better. The sources of information are much greater,
and the information itself is much more dependable. There have
been many advances in the art of security analysis. In all those
respects we are very far ahead of the past.

In one important respect we have made practically no progress at all, and that is in human nature. Regardless of all the apparatus and all the improvements in techniques, people still want to make money very fast. They still want to be on the right side of the market. And what is most important and most dangerous, we all want to get more out of Wall Street than we deserve for the work we put in.

There is one final area in which I think there has been a very definite retrogression in Wall Street thinking. That is in the distinctions between investment and speculation, which I spoke about at the beginning of this lecture. I am sure that back in 1914 the typical person had a much clearer idea of what he meant by investing his money, and what he meant by speculating with his money. He had no exaggerated ideas of what an investment operation should bring him, and nearly all the people who speculated knew approximately what kind of risks they were taking.

Today I find the situation is greatly confused in that regard, and nearly everybody participates in the confusion.

You call anything you wish an investment, particularly if you buy it outright--which for some months past you had to do anyway--yet nearly all the people think mainly in terms of price changes rather than of the income and of the intrinsic value.

The main requirement of success for Wall Street, I think-- viewing Wall Street as an institution now, and not only as a group of individual people--is a clarification of ideas as to the extent to which we can purchase securities under these widely fluctuating conditions and be reasonably satisfied, for logical reasons, that we are investing our money and not speculating. Once we can do that, then we can go back to a rational and a consistent policy of investment. And we shall be able to get people away from these speculative considerations and into sound investment policies, in spite of the wide fluctuations in the market which surround their operations. Finally when the intelligent investor elects to speculate, he will do it with his eyes open and a tendency to calculate his chances on a careful, businesslike basis.

These possibilities can be realized if you and I and the rest of us will only devote our skill and our intelligence to that end.

Thank you very much for your attention. (Applause)

End of Lecture #10, the last in the series.

****